VOID OF MOON

The Emotional Journey Through Marital Separation

by Denise Falcone

Published by Helm Publishing
Rockford, IL

**Void of Moon
The Emotional Journey
Through Marital Separation**

All Rights Reserved ©2005 by Helm Publishing
and the Author, Denise Falcone

No part of this book may be reproduced, or transmitted in any form or by any means, graphic, electronic, or mechanical, including photocopying, recording, taping, or by any information storage retrieval system, without the permission in writing from the publisher or the author.

Helm Publishing

For information:
Helm Publishing
3923 Seward Avenue
Rockford, Illinois 61108
www.publishersdrive.com

ISBN 0-9760919-6-8
Printed in the United States

*The epigraph for the chapter Sadness is reprinted with permission of Simon and Shuster Adult Publishing Group from SOME CAN WHISTLE by Larry McMurtry.
Copyright 1989 by Larry McMurtry*

This book is dedicated to my mother, who not once, but twice, embarked on this journey. You are an inspiration.

This map of my personal journey is dedicated to all women who took heart wrenching wrong turns because they had nowhere else to go and no one to follow.

The love that enabled me to write this book goes out to my daughter Gina, and to all the children in the world who need their mothers to do the right thing.

Acknowledgements

First of all, I would like to thank all of the people I contacted for permission to use their work, who blessed this book by getting back to me right away and wishing it well. I would like to thank the authors whose words inspired me and helped me along my path, and whose words will now help others.

I would like to thank my friends (you know who you are) for giving me unceasing encouragement with this project, even though I wouldn't let any of you read a word until it was finished.

Thank you Bill DeCandido for helping us creative people feel comfortable in that foreign place, where we do not understand or speak the language, but you do. You are a marvelous interpreter and a good friend.

Renee Infantino, your drawings are so beautiful. Your images add so much to the power of this book. Thank you for sharing so much of yourself and your talent with this project.

Thank you TJ Loughran for your dynamite ideas. Your designs for Void of Moon brought it to a new place, beyond the realization of my expectations. Working with you in all phases of putting this book together gave me the confidence to keep going on a level of integrity that I could only wish for.

Dianne Helm, where did you come from? Your inherent understanding of what this book is all about makes you a kindred spirit and a gift from heaven. Thank you for always being there for me as a publisher and as a friend.

At last, I want to thank my husband, Tim Evans, for reading every word I wrote and for urging me to keep going. You are my North Star.

Denise Falcone

Introduction

I wrote Void of Moon; The Emotional Journey Through Marital Separation because I felt that what had defined itself to me as a real emotional process warranted a map. When I found myself struggling and looking for help, I could not find such a map or a guide, so I was forced to create my own. My situation was mine alone and unique to me, but there were enough similarities to other women, who were sharing their experiences with me, that a guidebook of some sort seemed necessary.

Void of Moon makes important a map of a collective and connected passage for women who must end what began as a deep, romantic relationship hoped to last forever. Women seriously looking for the right direction on their journey seem to go back in time and draw from their dreams, because that is where we live. Yet, as reliable as the meanings of our dreams may be, survival through a struggling marriage that might end with separation requires enormous amounts of creativity and ideas at a time when there is no energy. Many women are likely to take a financial beating, and all of us must try to stay healthy in the meantime. To discover ourselves, so we can keep going, we are forced to dispel our illusions and at the same time live out our fantasies. This is a journey that can take a long time, sometimes years, because everyone must move at her own pace, and most of it is uphill. Is it worth it?

My hope for this book of emotional mapping is that it brings enlightenment through conflicting and urgent emotions, through foreign feelings and unrecognizable, sometimes uncontrollable reactions that begin to take hold and do not leave us. My experience has taught me that, in time, it is possible to move on from only reacting to these feelings, and eventually understand, thrive and grow beyond them. You might emerge touched very deeply by the results, and quite possibly be changed forever, one way or another, but you will live the rest of your life as you.

*The Moon
represents the internal
female influence, the emotions, and
innermost needs. Without the influence of
the Moon, we can suffer many emotional and
physical illnesses, which drain our energy and
prevent us from discovering our true inner selves.
The Moon
represents instincts and the mother. Separating from the
mother and discovering our own true nature apart from her
is essential for us to live a satisfying life, according to our own needs.
The Moon
is associated with romantic attraction and love.
The Moon's glow and pull towards romance awakens
our feminine, receptive selves. We gaze at the
night sky and we become moonstruck.*

When there is no Moon, there is darkness.
The healing power of the darkness can
only happen if we let go, surrender
to the chaotic void, and embrace the journey.

Contents

The Power of Change — 1

Confusion — 17

Confrontation — 33

Sadness — 49

The Coming of the Light — 67

Entrapments, Delays, and Stops — 85

Preparation and Planning — 103

Separation and Uncertainty — 125

The Power of Change

"We are volcanoes. When we women offer one experience as our truth, as human truth, all the maps change. There are new mountains."
Ursula K. Le Guin

I think to some degree everyone should learn to separate from others emotionally. People need to grow into themselves with as little mental baggage to tote around as possible. Our psychological destiny depends on it. For many women, marital separation, often leading to divorce, is the result of a determined attempt to move forward in this direction.

People who do not relate to each other, and are married, live a life that has silenced them. But since they say that our souls, our inner beings, are always working at growing and evolving until the day that we die, whether or not we are aware of it, needs that are not met in our lives, that help us to grow and evolve, can begin to manifest themselves in disruptive ways. Should you feel guilty about changing who you are in a relationship? It is through our relationships that we evolve. Although what we want is to evolve within the relationship, sometimes we cannot.

Making a decision to radically change your life, by separating from your spouse emotionally and physically, is a difficult one. It is the absolute shattering of the status quo. The beginning of this change could start with small feelings of discomfort, and then escalate into an extreme sense of impending doom. Yet it can feel tempting at the same time, often liberating, because you may be at a place where you want things to be different, no matter what, and separation might be the only way to make it happen. At this time, you could feel like you are being pulled in two directions at once, and it could be impossible to quiet the constant signals.

After years of struggling to find a common ground with my husband, I longed for a new self-image that was different from the image I consistently saw everyday when I looked in the mirror. Don't even ask me how I looked in photographs, or how I sounded when I spoke to him. There was I and the way that I felt. The facts were available for all to see, and hear, but I felt them. There was so much pain in my face. I heard my pissed-off voice, and I felt terrible every time I had to confront this reality. Whenever there were seemingly happy people around me, especially couples, I felt envious of them and sorry for myself, because I was settled into an immovable life with a future that was probably doomed to be lived unhappily, with someone whom I thought I loved. We were married, but we were not a couple anymore. What would happen to me? How could this have happened to us?

Our needs change, our tastes change and evolve as we do, or hope to do in our lives. It is easy to accept some changes. When our needs in a close relationship change, it can be very scary, especially when we discover that what it is we want, we want alone. Here we are, married to someone in the box but we are growing out of the box. This can be just annoying at first, and it can be easy to accept the contradictions because after all, that's life. Life is full of contradictions. Some marriages, for whatever reasons, can sustain comfortably through years of collisions and conflicts. When the contradictions and negations seem no longer acceptable, and we feel that we must pay attention to them as if bells were ringing all the time, we might be at the point where we indeed feel alone and impaired, after a time damaged and more discontented than ever. Our lives depend on a solution. For me, marriage was a solution. It was something promised and vowed to last forever, and it would make everything all right. The sacrament of this blessed union would solve, but now I was not too sure.

I hated it when people who met us for the first time were shocked to discover that we were a couple. "You guys are so different!" I felt embarrassed, and again and again confronted by what I was trying to deny on a daily basis. Yeah, yeah, yeah, I would say to myself, we are different. So what? Well, the fact that I was fighting against living alone, with my own set of values, desires and priorities was quite obvious. People who didn't even know us could notice this. I felt that I could not share anything with my husband except the things that he was interested in.

It feels like a big responsibility to realize this, and accept it, because the weight of this disenchantment is heavy, and again something that is yours alone to bear. Even when a part of you knows that you are growing in a positive direction, any direction away from the other person feels difficult. You walk around in circles saying that the problem is me, is me, is me, but when living with someone you once wanted to be with for the rest of your life begins to feel like living with an unwanted roommate, or a guest who stays too long, life can become horrible and difficult. It can start out feeling like it is your fault that it has become this way as well.

Deafening silence can dominate an atmosphere where two souls are no longer related. The ear-splitting realization that you have nothing to say to each other can act out in desperate ways. You may bang pots and pans, and slam doors and windows, just to get some noise. My husband and I had not been communicating to each other at all during one evening, yet I was determined to go about my business as usual. I cooked a very good dinner. When there was still no decent contact by the end of the meal, I was ready to burst with all sorts of pent up emotions, from days, and months and maybe even years of not relating gone by. I opened the window above the sink and began to fling the dirty dinner plates into the air like Frisbees. Whee! This one is for my anger! This one is because of my frustration with you and your goddamn behavior! This is how sad I feel about us; watch this one go! There goes your mother, out the window! I looked at my husband's horrified face. Finally, I had gotten my point across.

Hold it! This is not the way to go about reporting your feelings to anyone, not even to yourself. Although it was a release of a tremendous amount of bottled up frustration, it turned into something very sad as I watched him take the broom and dustpan out of the closet to go sweep up the ruins of my piece of mind. But where can we go when our problems come from the ones we love? We can first learn by our mistakes. If you can extend yourself through and beyond the nerve-racking quiet, you will begin to give yourself permission to accept the changes you feel with restraint, and without causing a riot. You do not have to understand everything right now.

Some partners threaten with abandonment, with verbal abuse, physical abuse or just plain sickening manipulation to make you feel like changing the way you want and need things to be in the relationship is wrong. It upsets them too much to go there with you. It is amazing: no matter how expansive a job some men might have, many still prefer to stay stuck in the same comfy, bed of roses routine at home. So, you are left all alone again. Upstairs, in the bathroom while you are shaving your legs, you are faced with a choice. You think that you are ready to set off on an emotional journey of separation. You will either be together or not be together. You are not going to take this shit anymore. If it is more of a worry about what kind of creature you might eventually become, or what kind of life you will live if you stay with the way things are now, rather than with your idea of becoming a separate person from him, however vague it seems to you now, you are here. Welcome aboard.

Amidst this change, while slipping in and out of states of disappointment and disillusionment, you will question the meaning of your marital destiny many times. You may watch many of the things you were once connected to suffer what feels like a brutal series of cruel executions and final curtains. You will suddenly remember events from the past, because the roles that you played and the effects it had on you then matters now. Days become a checklist of reminders: when you were angry, when you felt hurt, when you were unjustifiably left out in the cold, or when you were just turned off. This process of letting go is eventual and continuous. This is the beginning of something ending. This sad fact, which can be hard to accept right now, is even sadder if you feel that you and your spouse never even really had a fair chance to fulfill your promise together. So, you feel reluctant to separate, emotionally and physically.

You may have a difficult time feeling worthy enough to separate into yourself, and you may feel guilty about growing in your own direction. Leaving someone behind seems like a much more difficult path. You might begin to obsess about falling seriously ill, or harbor fears of dying. From this place of setting off to a place of not knowing what the future may bring, exiting through illness or death seems easier. From an overwhelming sense of helplessness, you might develop fears of the outside world. This is how fear of change can manifest itself.

One day I passed the home of a neighbor, who I knew was having a really hard time being married to her husband. She was sitting on her front stoop in shorts and a tee shirt, smoking like a chimney. I did not say anything to her since we were not friends; in fact I wasn't even sure if I liked her. But I will never forget the image of her sitting there. She looked terrible. Her face was drawn in and silent, and her eyes looked out towards me with the weight of the world on her shoulders. She looked so sad. How deep in my soul I knew how she felt at that very minute. My heart went out to her because she was part of the tribe. I, and many other women, could finish this story based on our own. After a while, she was going to put out her last cigarette and go back inside to join her family. She would check her determined thoughts about her survival on that stoop against what she would face when she got inside, do the dishes and go to bed. And pray that another irresolvable tomorrow never comes. That is what it is like on an all right day when you begin to think that you want to separate from your husband.

    Since there was nothing happening to me that was too serious health wise, except the stress from not being able to make things right in my life felt like it was killing me, I felt myself worried about getting older. Time seemed to race towards the wreck of me. I became more aware of my depressed state of mind, and I could not see a way out. I was becoming more adapted at speeding up the aging process, and I fell into a calling that propelled me towards the end of carrying this burden by abandoning all forms of anything that had to do with my wellbeing. I felt like saying who cares anymore? Give me those cupcakes over there. Let's go shopping. Then, I began to mourn the loss of everything I ever had to let go of in my entire life. I wanted second chances with all of it now. Life was turning into this heavy load of mistakes and loss to carry around with me every day. In addition, I was paying attention to every bad thing that existed in the world. I was the epitome of catastrophe because I was scared of messing things up.

Good Mother or Bad Mother? Or Both?

It is easy to suffer all of the responsibility for the impact your decision to separate will have on your spouse and the rest of the family, especially if you are a mother. That alone will keep many women in a marriage that they do not want to be in anymore. A woman might assume the role of parenting her spouse, whether it is wanted or not, to make up for the kind of parenting which her spouse, or she, may not have had in life. We set off to fill in the cracks and set the tone as soon as we take our vows. We make it a nice warm nest and start married life off all tucked in. We don't dare bother to stir things up because we might wake the baby, the baby being the relationship because are we really sure our spouse needs all that mothering? The baby will cry, maybe even have a tantrum. God forbid.

In the past, that approach might have worked for me. For years. But then, I had to become the bad mother. My attempts to make some noise, from citing the reasons why I freak out on a daily basis, by stating the month, day and time for instances and examples of when and why I was peeved, to prompt the relationship to be the way that I needed it to be, failed miserably at my expense. I tried everything. If you are in changing mode now, you have to switch into the bad mother too. It is one of the last resorts. Change comes from chaos, right? If you receive no satisfaction or positive results from doing this, except reactions of blaming, yelling, lashing out and all of that other unpleasant stuff expected from much younger children, it is time to give up the role of the good mother and the bad mother, and just let the baby cry in the crib. You might as well at this point be you. Hopefully, the baby will grow up. Maybe the baby doesn't want to grow up. Do you have the courage to see it for what it is, this thing that you gave birth to? Then what? It is also important to remember that good parenting does not quench the soul, stopping it from growing, like the ancient custom of binding the feet. That kind of parenting binds the soul. Good parenting awakens the soul, feeds it, enlivens it and gives it what it needs to grow, to separate from the mother and to find and own it's self. But people have to recognize and put their trust in that sensibility.

My parents did not always see the way to be parents and they made some mistakes. Thank you very much. But, that's ok. Everyone has life to contend with. As a reaction to some of my husband's childhood experiences, I played the role of the good mother, trying hard at being generally charming and perfect, and feeling his head for fever on a regular basis. Then, my part got switched at his convenience, with a snap of his fingers, into the role of the bad, uncontrollable, ungrateful little girl. It was his turn now. "You bought a coat without me, you greedy insufferable thing! You only married me for my money." What money? This routine did not work well at all to enhance, erase, or fix either of our childhood memories, nor did it do very much for our relationship. I did not want to play house with him anymore. I did not want to live in a reincarnation of my parents, or his. My parents did not even want to live in a reincarnation of themselves! Once was enough for everybody. I wanted something different from this relationship to move on to and grow from, and I realized that he did not. Nothing I could do would drag my husband away from his modus operandi. I had finally realized how lonely I was, but for what?

The power of change can be over-whelming. Instead of languishing and wasting away in its awe, you can advance, and move through it, whether you stay in the marriage or not. It depends on your state of mind. We are often so grateful for our ability just to survive through life, that we stop right there. We mark ourselves proudly as survivors, and then limit ourselves from the rest of it. We become stuck in survival. We should not just survive. We should keep going way beyond that. People are living longer these days, and staying young in the meantime. There is a world of possibility out there. People who have no hopes and dreams outside of survival have nowhere to go on life's journey. They make no accomplishments in life. There might be material things to accumulate, and the living for and through one's children, but to have just that is one layer of a life that can be deeply rewarding in so many other ways. But then we might lose what we have now. The terror of the unknown is strong. It can make you want to crawl away and hide under the bed, but protecting yourself from the unforeseen is much harder work, and it takes its toll. You will be too tired all the time, feel ill and depressed, while you think that you are protecting yourself from life when you are really avoiding it.

One day in my old house, there was a fresh, unopened bag of chips on the kitchen counter, tempting me beyond belief to rip it open and eat all of its contents right then and there. All of the satisfaction I ever needed from my life at that moment could be contained in one ever so brief eating-spell of what was inside that bag. It would have taken me three minutes to devour its delicious contents, and the fulfillment from doing so would have lasted four. Or, I could have gone to a yoga class. I certainly needed it. And not stay at home, feeling guilty all night about stuffing myself with a bag of salty chips, and worse than that, feeling too guilty to go to yoga class because I was convinced that I had to stay home to take care of my healthy, absolutely resourceful if need be family, who had a full refrigerator and the warmth of a home at their disposal.

Later that day…

I made my decision. Little human faces, with great big eyes, peeked out of an opening in the front door, watching me leave as if I were going into quarantine and might never come back. My guilt about leaving them for a couple of hours suddenly loomed over me as a huge phantom creature in a long, black, flowing robe. It asked me in a low, foreboding voice, "What if you don't come back?"

Everyone had these abandonment issues over a one-and a half hour yoga class. Everyone, including me, had this going away feeling whenever I wanted to do something like this.

So many married women are conditioned to feel punished for the decisions they make to enrich their lives. We either have a defensive attitude about it when we do it, or we just don't do it to alleviate everyone else's discomfort about it. If we go somewhere without them, perhaps we will be reprimanded for our leaving by yet another cruel twist of fate, and get hit by a bus on the way. And it will be our fault entirely.

When we project our own feelings of helplessness onto others, we become frozen in a time of guilt. We also resent these people we are putting ourselves out for, no matter how much we love them and sincerely want to be there for them always, or feel it is our obligation to be there for them all the time. We even let their influence enter our thoughts. We think what they want us to think, and we manage to find no time for our own thoughts and feelings. Sometimes, we feel too much shame about our feelings to think them at all because they are separate thoughts. We put ourselves off and blame it on the needs of everyone. We think that we forget our needs and desires out of a sense of duty, but there is no real cause that should prohibit us from being ourselves, and from being accepted for who we are. Feeling entitled to a compromise from others, especially our loved ones, and a profession of our choice, not just a job, but also a way of being, to live in a way that helps us to grow into better and happier people, nurtures us.

★

We ask our partners in many different ways if they are with us, support us, believe us, *oh please believe us*, and if they will join us in life or not, and we experience feelings of disappointment and self-doubt when they prefer to stand outside. Ok, stand outside. At least I can see you out there in my field of vision, even if it is outside, even if it is outside of me. I can see you through the window. We can continue to look for love through a microscope and wonder if it will ever multiply, become something and be fruitful, and perhaps blossom. At this stage of your journey, the thought of not being with your spouse anymore, to face even the possibility of not being able to fold his socks and underwear and put them in the drawer anymore, can be more than disappointing. It can paralyze you, and it can feel like the end of the world. You will want to avoid that at all costs.

Fear of separating can outweigh the reasons why you want to leave. You can get lost in many different feelings and fears. You may hate this risk, this whole stupid idea. What was I thinking, you might ask yourself? What a fool I am, am I crazy? You may feel that you want everything to go back to the way it used to be, before all of this nonsense about you and your needs. This is normal. Change is hard.

Confusion

"When people are taken out of their depths they lose their heads, no matter how charming a bluff they may put up."
F. Scott Fitzgerald

Feeling confused and giving in to the voicelessness and vulnerability it can cause can pull you down, so keeping yourself up on a daily basis is like treading water. It takes a lot of strength to do this, instead of giving in to drowning. By transforming your scattered disobedience and chaos into a focused state of mind, towards what is plainly and simply positive and the better way to go about things, you can emerge through this time of change. Although you might feel confused and lost about everything you have ever known right now, you can attain the staying power and confidence to keep going if you try to stay in the present. Keep following that on a day-to-day road as you search for your course. The right way for you to go will unfold gradually, and eventually, if you want it to and when you are ready.

Do not rush or fight through this time. This is not the part of the story when you run in to the bedroom, pack your bags, and flush your wedding ring down the toilet. Unless you suddenly become aware that you are being physically abused on a regular basis, reacting this way will not send your emotions away; it will only make your life more complicated and unpleasant. Wait for more clarity. You are just becoming awakened to a new state of your mind. Let go of a desperate need to act on your feelings, to prove and to punish, and allow yourself to be carried through with the tide and pace of your confusion. There is always something for you to learn along the way. Here is your opportunity to allow yourself the chance to understand more about your relationship.

Separating from another and into you is a process of letting go and growing. Here you are, someplace you want to be and don't want to be, with unexplainable and unwanted feelings all the way around. Fear of what will happen tomorrow can loom terrific and tremendous in this state of mind. You can feel quite powerless over your fate because you have just entered into, and became aware of yourself, in this strange new place.

Fear of breaking up the family...the impact it will have on the children...fear of repeating what you are going through now...being alone...feeling lonely…the impact on the extended family…growing old alone…raising young children alone…labels…lack of money…quality of childcare…single life…starting over…staying healthy…avoiding stagnation… pride…These concerns are before you now without resolve.

Carrying on in a state of not knowing is not as easy as most people out there in the world make it look. Be one of the intelligent ones. Stop, look, and listen. This is your mantra. Be receptive to the knowledge that you can receive now. When you are confused, the long view ahead can be dark and terrifying, but when one sees from day to day, it can become easier to integrate it into possibility. See from day to day now and collect the data in the meantime. Can you let go of your fears of the uncertain future for a while, and just sit back and observe today?

Your marriage is the factory from which most of your habits and daily grind emerge. When you feel confused about your main source of enrichment, you might feel lost and guideless. You may not feel as grounded as you have felt back in the good old days, and you might start to fear the loss of something real and important. The frightening realization that my name might not hold up to anything anymore without the oomph of M.R.S. before it, that marvelous, powerful, open sesame that conveyed to the world that I had arrived, made me feel like I was at world's end. What if this marriage might actually not be the way I thought to a life worth living? Now what? These thoughts sent me reeling into a sea of unworthiness and panic. I felt like my life raft was being deflated. The shades were being drawn. Doors would start to close on me. Where will I go now and who will I feel entitled to be?

When we are confused, we naturally feel that we must react and urgently discover what is going on, and then we work too hard to know. This is because it is always easier to do what we are used to doing, the chicken without a head dance; thrashing and running around all over the place in a constant state of not knowing, showing our fears by the minute. We do this over little, non-essential things. Imagine how we act out when something as significant and large as our marriage and livelihood are being threatened?

The best thing to do when you feel confused is to stop. Instead of reacting to feelings of helplessness, which causes tremendous discomfort and the urgency to act, stop and try to listen to your inner voice, which is often a gentler, more compassionate signal. Live in the present now. This is not the time to control everything that has happened in the past, or is it the time to control everything that has not even happened yet. Stop!

Quieting ourselves is always a good way to hear our inner voices. This time of confusion is a good time to focus on things that can help you to relax, and focus your thoughts on what counts. Don't try so hard now. Work at doing your job, whatever that may be, and let the uncomplicated details of your life be what you mainly focus on right now. Use these activities to pull yourself back from what you do not understand. This is not the time to mourn for the loss of anything before it happens.

There are healthy ways to pass this time. Here are some suggestions:

Meditation allows you to be in touch with your inner self. It opens your mind to receiving psychic, spiritual information and energy. It helps to clear your mind of thoughts, fears and anxieties, and it can help to lower your blood pressure. It helps you to learn total relaxation.

Exercise helps you to bring more energy to yourself. If performed first thing in the morning, it sets the tone for the whole day. Exercise helps you to stay in the present, helps to slow down the aging process, and relieves you of the burden of having to think all the time.

Creative pursuits are a way to your inner world. No matter how simple or difficult, old or new, who is to judge? Just do it.

This is a good time to be more outside of you. Take a break from yourself and let yourself expand............... Take advantage of a chance to escape into another world for a while. Make yourself more interesting.

Dream.

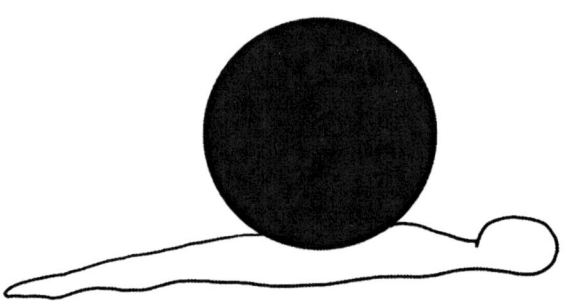

"If a little dreaming is dangerous, the cure for it is not to dream less but to dream more, to dream all the time."

Marcel Proust

Write down your dreams. Dreams provide a window for you to see into your deep unconscious mind, especially now, when things are being all stirred up. You are guided to that part of yourself through the many images you project, while your soul is speaking. When you pay attention to the messages, you can begin to understand them and start to disarm. You could even begin to heal your past. When you avoid your dreams, intuition and your inner voices, you inhibit your power to move forward.

Panic attacks can start to occur when we feel lost, afraid and vulnerable, and these unfortunate episodes can happen, and probably will, at the worst possible times. These are scary moments. Loss of memory can occur. Out of body experiences can materialize. Open the windows and breathe. Here is a certainty. If you are alive and feel no longer protected by everything that is set up outside of yourself, you are going to be afraid. You might even be terrified. Terrified! What will happen if we really do let our fears go all out and watch our ramparts fall apart? We might be left standing with all of our facades and pretenses lying about like crashed ruins at our feet. And there we are!

I found myself being unable to drive on busy roads and highways. Bridges were out of the question for me. Once or twice, I had to pull over to the side. I forgot what time I had to get my daughter off to school, and I had to look up my friend's phone numbers again. I constantly worried that I was going crazy. I was losing control of my life, and becoming mad and hysterical because of the feeling of no way out. Then, other women began to come out of the woodwork, and shared their panic attack experiences with me. The fact that these experiences happened to others as well made me feel a little better. I was not alone in the world. This made me more compassionate to the people sticking me the finger, and honking their horns when I drove too slowly, or when I took too long to move from the changing traffic light. I began to understand that other people had problems too.

Some people take tranquilizers, or other drugs and substances to cope with this predicament, this feeling of extreme vulnerability to change, because fears and disorders manifest themselves physically here. I remember sitting with some women around the baby pool one long, very hot summer. The children were so cute in their little bathing suits. The mothers were attentive, each mom in her own special way. All of us felt good about giving our kids sunny days at the pool with friends. Towels were cheery in design, and draped over chaise lounges, and raw carrots, chocolate milk and fresh baby bottles emerged from clean, brightly colored coolers. Then, I became shocked to realize that these mothers were stowing sea breeze cocktails in those coolers also. Peeking under the surface of that so-called innocent scene from my lofty perch, were they guilty? Women need to function, sometimes no matter what.

In one of my daily hallucinations, I watched the whole world functioning in one big revolving panic attack. I thankfully discovered my fear of getting caught and taken prisoner in these places of beyond having fun, of instability, too many cigarettes, possibly dependent on drugs or alcohol, legal insanity, endless shopping, self-induced ugliness and self hatred, than where I actually was, which was really only in a paralyzed state of fear and dread. With this understanding, I was able to find the confidence to stop worrying so much. Everyone was running scared and so was I. Join the motivated by fear club. So much of how we survive is because of fear. This shake-up and revolution is the start of self-observation and self-renewal, and the way to see who you really are, and who you are becoming as you mature.

When you find you, and accept yourself, you can begin to let go of some of the rest. Practice letting go by starting with material things, and silly, superficial emotional attachments to things that should not matter to you anymore, or bring you down. How much more stuff and nonsense must we accumulate and hold on to because we do not have enough of others, or ourselves? Let go of some of those present-day encumbrances and old played out memories. Lighten your load. Maybe they will stop haunting you. How much more can we blame our husbands, our family, our fourth grade teachers, that perverted old uncle who is probably dead now anyway, and even the Deity, before we look at ourselves and say, well, maybe now it's up to me? If you continue on the endless search for things other than your real cause, you will miss the most valuable discovery of all, and that dwells inside of you. Do you remember her?

*

Why do so many women wait until they excel at all the wrong things before they give themselves permission to change their discontented lives into lives worth living? We blow ourselves up into big gusts of wind, declare war on everyone and everything and shoot the sparrows down with our great big shotguns. We give ourselves permission to wreak havoc all over the place, yet we cannot find whatever it takes to go after what we really want. We are even afraid to say what we really want. We are even afraid to think what we really want. Someone might hear us. We might hear us. Often the only places we give ourselves the right to say anything we feel are non-threatening, back-booths in diners, isolated coffee klatches sworn to secrecy or in expensive therapy sessions.

When I thought of finding myself again because I lost so much of myself trying to pursue and prove what I know now to be trivial and way outside of me, I remembered when I was a child how self-contained I could be. Whether it was just sitting on a rock like a turtle, examining moss or playing with my toys in my room, the world seemed to be revolving comfortably out there, outside of me, and I felt safe. When I became an adult, with grown up responsibilities and problems, the world crashed down my door, barged right in and I found myself more defenseless than I thought I was, or would like to admit that I was. Lucky for me for the appetizers and open bar:

Affairs… …Denial… …Drugs… …Food…

…Work… …Illness… …Magic Thinking…

…Depression… …Shopping…

…Alcohol… …Sainthood…

A life worth living is a life that can stand up to just about anything that tries to interrupt it, or pull it down. Sometimes, we believe that the evil eye or fate is preventing us from living life our way. If we are reasonably kind, we naturally do not want to hurt people, so we reluctantly remain prisoners of unfortunate circumstances, with one rebellious toe pointed out the door. Our lives are incomplete. If the things we desire are withheld from us often enough, we will begin to believe that we do not deserve them. If we are told things about ourselves often enough, we become believers of what we are told about ourselves.

If you start to feel that you are a victim of someone's inferior thoughts or deeds, it is possible that they are projecting their own fears and hatred about themselves onto you. You do not have to take part in this anymore when you want your life to change. This is why it is important to take you out of the picture and observe. No one will fall apart, or shrivel up and die, although you may secretly wish that they would, if only for a brief moment. The show will always go on, with or without you, but sit in the audience this time. When you watch the play and realize lots of things that turn out to be true because you can see and hear them with your own eyes and ears now from where you sit, and when you are able to accept these things as they truly are, rather than how they affect you, you are no longer a victim. You can choose to be no longer available and exit stage right or left. When you step outside of it all, your life may not be as exciting as it was before, but you might feel calm. Your life may not be as dramatic as it was before because you might stop needing to act out against so many things. Your life may not be as tragic as you thought it would be because you might find yourself, and you might not be so helpless after all. It is a loss of sorts, but a loss of something you thought you needed but never did. Then, what you thought would absolutely be the most catastrophic thing to ever happen to you, like feeling detached from all of it, may suddenly loose its power.

Anxiety about a relationship that might soon end, and the fear of being left alone to wade through the loss of what we once thought was everything, can causes us to deceive and pretend. Was I not already alone, lost to others and to myself through my self-deception and wishful thinking? I was not ready to face that fact, let alone make such a grand move into the present. I could not even begin to think of what it would take to do that. So, I kept myself safe in my denial, and I went through the motions of collecting all these things to fulfill my past, and coveted all the many different images I desired to add to my busy lifestyle of being someone else.

You may weigh what you care most about against other things. If your true self wins out, you may just have to accept your decision, and give in to the work involved to get you to that new place where you wish to be someday. You might be faced with the task of becoming someone else, someone new and different to everybody, and everybody might not like you anymore. Yes, you will probably have to leave a lot behind. People will shake their heads with sorrow and say that you have changed.

✶

    Besides a husband, I had a lot of furniture, a large apartment with a formal dining room, tables and chairs, silver-plate, pots and pans, television sets, plants, plans for the holidays whether I liked it or not, Christmas presents, birthday gifts, anniversary mementos, a child! and I knew what to expect every single day. It seemed like a lot of trouble to move all this stuff, to think about it and reevaluate it, and to change all of it around, all these things that were glued to this marriage. Marriage offers us the convenience of not having to think about these things, especially if you have a large garage. Things accumulate, and we take for granted that they are just a part of us that we take along. These things that we collect and store help to make our marriage visible, to others and ourselves.

    Sometimes we want to pass over the process of living because we do not trust ourselves to get through it well enough, or at all. We detour, and jump all over the place in a constant state of avoidance, keeping ourselves entrapped in the same, outdated, worn out images of ourselves. The traveling to get to someplace can be more difficult than living in the place of our arrival, no matter how foreign the sought out land is. There is baggage to carry and move about, strange neighborhoods, languages, and laws to adapt to, and most of all, the fear of getting lost on the way, all by ourselves.

It is important to try to find stability, balance and poise in a state of confusion. It is in this state of feeling lost that we are offered the opportunity to practice attainment of these strengths, and in practice we might eventually own them. Wisdom for you to carry on this journey is there if you want to find that also. Do not judge the source from whence it comes. The clearest understanding could come from a place that you least expect it would, while a sure fount of knowledge could disappoint you. This is why it is so important to allow your defenses and expectations to come down when you are searching for enlightenment and a way to proceed. If you have a goal in mind as an end to your journey or not, with the strength from what you took the time and made the effort to know each day, you will learn that it is the journey to the place that you want to go that counts.

Without accomplishing a sense of balance to live with day to day, here in a confused state of mind, you might jump all over the place from feeling uncomfortably torn apart in a million different directions. You could fall into the trap of an angry state, repressed or otherwise, with mucho resentment to get you through. You will harbor ill will towards everything because you do not understand. You face the danger of living in a state of denial and disease. It is the darkness without knowing, without any light at all. Unless you can begin to let go of your personal attachments to what keeps you down, you will lose the opportunity to live in a state of confusion, admit that you are here, and then gain the valuable insight and grounding skills you will need during what is probably the next stop on this passage you are on; the inevitable, uncomfortable presence of that which eventually emerges in any relationship that needs to change and grow.

Confrontation

"I was angry with my friend:
I told my wrath, my wrath did end.
I was angry with my foe:

I told it not, my wrath did grow."
William Blake

Fear of disappointing our partners, fear that we may be wrong, causing conflict and endangering the marriage, hurting our partner's feelings or making them angry often silences us. Some partners may block topics that are important to us and to the relationship for their own reasons. Our true voices disappear, and we end up adopting a submissive, holding-in, self-silencing behavior. You may start to do something about your feelings now. You may begin to react. You may not want to touch your partner anymore, and you may act on those feelings. Sex might stop now.

Confronting that special someone can cause the most terrible arguments where no one is listening but the neighbors. It was embarrassing and humiliating for me to think that every time I walked out of my house for a quart of milk, I would be recognized as the wife of that couple that fights all the time. Although what we did in our apartment was none of anyone's business, the sound of our squabbles must have been like a boom box to their ears. When we first try to let our own voices return and we hear them, we are often shocked to hear that they are loud, angry voices. Confrontation can be very scary.

Fighting can be a way to stay together. It is a sad ritual that two people will act out with each other again and again when they feel the need to connect. My husband had the most fantastic talent for getting me to perform. Whenever the wind would start to blow, the orchestra would begin to play and he would step up to revisit his podium, and once again wave his wand in conducting a pitiful requiem for us. The music was mesmerizing, and touched and opened all of my old wounds, and I twirled, and twirled around incoherent and raving in my desperate choreography. The longer he stood there, waving his big fat stick, silent and hard of hearing, the louder I sang my pleas, and the more readily I got into the act. I tried every mad method I could think of in those days, to try to change my discontentment into some sort of compromise.

After years of falling into hysterics this way, I was simply tired. It is heart wrenching to look back to see where I let myself go with my frustrations, and I cringe when I think about it today. When we discover and begin to feel the power of our fury, we can fall under the misjudgment that moving around out of sorts, and rolling around in the dirt to gain someone's attention will strengthen us. This delusion, that my acting out would change him, or even enlighten him a little about what his behavior did to me, that this carrying on with him in this way because I was unhappy would force things to be different, completely weakened me.

Anger can feel good upon awakening to it, especially if you have been numb to your emotions for a long time. Many years ago, when we were newlyweds, we had a fight. I hid myself in the bedroom with the lights out. I refused to eat the dinner that he had cooked for me. I felt angry and disappointed. He ran in to where I lay curled up in a ball on the bed and begged me to come out. I refused because I was furious with him and with whatever he did, and I could not even tell you what that was now. But most of all, it was good to feel my anger after years of repressing it. I did not want to let that feeling go just yet. I felt exhilarated with its power. I had been waiting all these years to feel the strength of this emotion. My fury put me in a position of feeling powerful and in charge. He sounded desperate and scared. This was a perfect opportunity to over react to what he had done, to feel submerged in my anger, even though I might drown, and let this poor guy take the rap. I will sometimes think with regret about my choice at that moment, of not getting up from that cold, dark bed on that night, where he sat on the floor pleading with me to come and eat a warm dinner. After years of my running away from confrontation, and then retreating into its seduction like an addict, he stopped chasing me. I will always wonder what would have happened if I had taken his hand, and let him lead me out of the darkness, out of my anger, and into the dining room to eat.

    Disturbing the peace can feed the relationship if that is what the relationship needs for it to continue. If the fighting stops, so might the relationship. Until we are ready to face that risk, we keep playing out our same old destructive roles, especially if that is all we have left. Sometimes people need the familiarity of the fighting, the closeness, the intimacy of it, especially if that is the only way left to connect. You might be offered the opportunity to connect in that way many times, and you might be tempted to accept that opportunity over and over again, rather than be alone. If you begin to try to address your problems in a more separate way, as a more separate individual, your partner might feel threatened.

If you refuse all of the blame that is being served up to you on a silver platter, if you try to initiate a new, healthier way of relating to each other simply by saying in a rational way - that this does not just belong to me, this belongs to you too, let's talk - this may cause more anger.

The effects of ranting and raving can be quite shocking. There is nothing worse than watching uncontrolled hostility do its thing. Yet, if we look around and listen to the sights and sounds of the world, it's all over the place. I kept having visions of myself running down Main Street in my underwear, bearing a hatchet. How can you separate yourself from your anger? If you can confront your past and realize that how you were made to feel as a child can effect your anger now, you can start to separate from those feelings. You are entitled to your anger, but anger directed at your partner can be a means of working out your past. It then becomes a two-folded place of dealing with anger: your past and your present. When your partner is angry with you, you need to remember what impact anger directed toward you had on you as a child. You need to confront your past to understand the meaning and impact of anger as it affects you now. This understanding can allow someone to be angry with you without you becoming paralyzed by its power.

There were times when my husband would not talk to me, and whenever I tried to make eye contact with him he would avert his gaze. What did I do? What did I do? My self-esteem would suddenly shrink down to the size of a pea. Oh, but I would often drop him like a hot potato too, when I felt irritated at him about something. It is so much easier to do that, to just cover the issues up with big white sheets and go on vacation. I will always feel sorry that we could not sit down, or take a walk and talk about our relationship. When things are bothering me, my need to talk to resolve it is strong. Although I just had to tell him about what perturbed me, so that we, or I, might find a solution and get on with our lives, he was often not ready to discuss it with me. Held back from talking and I turn into a Jimmy Swaggert type. Days of relating like this led to nothing but living in a state of no peace, no solutions, tons of antagonism towards each other, and the very unmarried feeling of alienation. If you think that this is bad, and it was, wait for the time when you really say the hell with the dirty rat.

Why do we marry these people? Since we are born into families, but are eventually meant to live our own lives, we have the first and most fertile opportunities to test out our social ambitions with our nearest and dearest. It can be the most comfortable place to work things out, especially if there is a fair amount of unconditional love conveyed towards us from our loved ones that we feel confident about. We don't mind testing out our wings, just in case we fall. If we have managed to leave the nest, but still need to learn how to fly, and this is much like most of us, our choice in subjects will usually extend from where we started until we learn.

★

Standing up for yourself and expressing anger to others in a healthier way can evoke feelings of separateness and aloneness in you, which can feel very scary at first. You begin to cut the tangled, knotted mess that keeps you comfortably and safely entwined. We should not only learn to accept our anger, but we need to learn to channel our anger, so it can be expressed in a better way. Expressing anger in a way that is direct and rational is hard to do at a time when we feel helpless, vulnerable and ignored. All respect and consideration disappears when anger is out of control and misdirected.

Here I am again, shrieking and yelling, yelling and shrieking, slamming the door, throwing things on the floor, breaking glass, taking unwanted and dangerous walks alone at night to get away, entertaining horrible thoughts of revenge…and in addition to all of that, I was feeling retroactive anger about my past. I could just about understand the acts of murderous rage that put some women in the headlines. I was nuclear. I was covered with it.

Standing up for yourself, no matter how wretched you appear to yourself and others, can help you to become stronger and more trusting of your own true feelings. Eventually, you might feel more entitled to your anger. You are finally letting it out. You don't have to bury your angry feelings like smelly rags because you feel ashamed and frightened of them. Anger does exist and if it is your state of mind, you need to listen to that, and respect it. Anger is as real an emotion as any thing else, and you are entitled to it.

Great feats of strength have been accomplished with the courage anger can evoke. If you can stay in control of your rational self, and be focused on and true to your reasons for being pissed off, you can use it as tool to get you to a new, better place where you are afraid to go. That is so much better than staying put in the going on about the whole thing, again, and again, and again. The problem is not that you are angry, but how you express your anger. When you lose the shame and the terror attached to feelings of anger, you allow yourself to hear the screaming and hollering as the desperate attempt that it is, yours and everyone else's, clean and clear. Listen, as horrible as it may sound.

A new voice emerges from a woman when she is confident and secure with her feelings. Feeling entitled to whatever feelings she has, even her anger, gives her a more grounded, clearer voice to communicate to others with. In loosing the fear from her voice, she looses her status as shrew, scold, bitch, hothead, spoiled, selfish-child, man-eater and nag.

✶

    Strength for coping with and controlling your anger, especially your unfocused, uncensored anger, is developed and advanced in your decision not to always give in to the rage, no matter how enticing it might be. Yes, there is always just one more thing that you could say, *hold on, I'll get the list*, and taking yourself out of an argument that is going nowhere, accept probably to a bad end, is very hard. But this is the rocky road that you are on now. Keep walking and dodge the land mines that are waiting for you. There is all this stuff finally surfacing now. Things that you have always wanted to say are coming out with the courage that your anger has bestowed on you. There are many masochistic temptations on your part to react and examine all of it, rather than just leave it alone and walk away. Rage and lashing out is easier, so much more immediate, momentarily more gratifying, but it is in the walking away that we save others who are with us, such as our children, and ourselves from harm.

Confrontation between two people who are unhappily married is draining. It can hurt. It's invasive. It can chip away at your defenses before you are ready to let them down. You may begin to feel the weariness caused by watching all respect and dignity fly out the window, along with the other things that you might have been tossing out there as well. (I was infamous for throwing things out of the window.) Then, one day you catch a sideways glimpse of reality and see yourself as too tired to fight anymore. You might also take note of feelings of shame and alienation, brought on by feeling responsible for a failed relationship. You might begin to see an inventory of your losses now. You might start to feel the results of your holding on to the myth that marriage automatically brings the state of living happily ever after. There might be the realization that the very connection that you have been fighting so hard to keep, at the expense to yourself, is falling apart. This relationship has not developed in the way that you wanted it to, or thought it would. These are strong realizations. Rather than take this all in straight on, you might just prefer to stay mad.

Whenever I would try to let go of my anger, I would feel like I wasn't doing my job. Like scrubbing the floor and doing the wash, being the angry one in my marriage was part of my labor contract. It was when I had to promise my frightened out of her wits three-year old daughter that Mommy would no longer act like a maniac, that I had to seek a better way to be employed. My husband would have to adjust to the let down he felt when I wouldn't allow myself to be a victim of his childish goading, and his need to see me lower myself, especially in front of her. This was the walking through the end of my rancor. My sweet, innocent child inspired me to behave as a reasonably sane adult, and to tell you the truth, letting some of that tension and frenzy go from my life felt like I had finally taken off my girdle after a really long day.

Here we go…here comes, what for many of us are, the dreaded weekends. Everybody is home. A good way to stop the toxic waste from spilling all over the place is to start with embracing the fact that everyone is going back to work on Monday. The busy week will begin again. Ignore most of the traps that are going to be set up for you, and avoid the ones that you always seem to set up for yourself. Try your best not to pay so much attention to the bothersome things that you know you are capable of ignoring if you put your mind to it. If you feel tempted to call the lawyer right now and it is Sunday afternoon, realize that it is not through anger alone that you solve the problems of your marriage, or because of that you leave. It is through our anger that we come to the realization that something is wrong. The noise of our unhappiness announces this to us plain and clear.

Eventually, you should move beyond your anger for more insight into your relationship, whether you want to separate physically from your spouse or not. Let the poison of your anger finally neutralize into strength and wisdom for hope for the better now, and get busy doing something good. Everyone is entitled to a good weekend. Refuse the bad vibes. Know that it is bad for all of you. Walk out of the house if you need to, but remember not to slam the door. Getting down to daily, mundane priorities gives everyone a chance to cool down and forget sometimes. Go have the car washed, and maybe by some miraculous, divine, extraordinary intervention, all will move beyond the crap and the hellish inventions, and even surrender to a cease-fire, rather than give in to a new battle tomorrow.

Living in an environment of constant, unresolved anger is lethal for the mental, and physical health of everyone who lives there, especially the children. There are more acts of rage today because people do not know what to do with all of their anger. It's like garbage. People just do not know where to put it anymore. Children are brought up on this cruel gruel. The violent language and reactions today, including the stuff that comes out of our kids, is appalling and it is beyond belief that it could actually get to this low point in our society. Uncontrolled, unresolved anger is over-flowing into our world. Like the blob. Do you want to keep legitimizing your misdirected anger, so your children can learn to feel and act out just like you, and learn to solve, (or not to solve), their problems this way? Honk your horn just one more time.

Using your children to seek out revenge or retaliation against your partner, using them as an extension of your hatred, and playing them as pawns in a very poor unsportsmanlike game of getting back is a crime, and a form of child abuse, as you poison their minds with your unwanted trash. It is also a stupid crime against yourself because you will never feel good about doing this, no matter how many good digs you get in, and this kind of injustice will come back to haunt you someday, sooner or later. In the meantime, you are hurting your children the most. Why not take it as a task to teach your children how to understand anger, explain why you feel angry and impatient with the limitations and shortcomings of people, and why people act out poorly in anger. Teach them how to deal with their own anger, and how to protect themselves from it. They will surely need those skills in this world we live in today. This is our responsibility, and we owe this to our children.

When you stand up, clear-headed and rational, to protect you and your children from the effects of rage, regardless of the fact that you are shaking in your boots from the fear of it, the result of this unselfish and courageous act is that you eventually, through hard and unceasing practice, become that strong person that you are pretending to be. You can stick your head into the lion's mouth and emerge with intuition and understanding, rather than with injury. When you are able to take yourself out of an angry state, become more rational, and take such action in your own behalf, you will become more confident when it is safer and better to remove yourself from it, and you will find the strength and determination to do so.

One day my husband employed our daughter into one of his demented schemes to make me look bad so he could look good. As usual, he succeeded. But my angry words and ugly face, with the spit flying all over the place when I talked, were not enough of an outlet for me to express how I felt because I really wanted to kill him, (so to speak of course). Nor was that stunning image of myself that I projected enough of a threat to make him stop. You would think that it would have made him run. So, drunk with fury, I picked up one of our dining room chairs and threw it at him, while he continued to whisper things about me into her ear while holding her in his arms. That was it. I was done. This was the day, it was a Sunday morning and I will never forget it, (it seems like it is always on a Sunday morning, doesn't it?) when I decided never to let his unloving, self-serving contrivances get into me and fuel my rage like this again. When I saw that chair fly through the air towards my daughter, I vowed that I would use that very strength that I found to hurl it like it weighed nothing, to pull off what I, until now, thought was impossible. I was going to separate myself from him.

✶

If you can acknowledge and embrace the uncertainty of what lies beyond your anger, you will discover new aspects and dimensions of yourself. When you come to terms with and face your anger, you can let it go, give it up, and move forward. Anger is a strong drug. It intoxicates us and makes us feel important and visible.

You need to move on from a state of anger if you want to grow. You will no longer have it as an excuse to stay put in its safe harbor. You have to let go of your addiction to bitterness, but why wouldn't you want to? You can finally let go of the blaming, and climb out of that low level of existence. When you let go of the lashing out and put out the fire, you free yourself from living a life of violence and turmoil. When you let go of your anger and let it evolve into reason and sanity, you will feel more separate from it, even when you feel anxious and invisible. You begin to get ready to open up and accept to heart some deeper feelings…

Sadness

"The lives of happy people are dense with their own doings—crowded, active, thick…But the sorrowing are nomads, on a plain with few landmarks and no boundaries; sorrows horizons are vague and its demands few."
Larry McMurtry, Some Can Whistle

We get ourselves into gear to face our confusion, fears, and rage, and meet those feelings when we must. We can do that. For many of us, those feelings have been waiting in the wings for us to cue them to come forth and finally be released. We postpone feeling sad though, sometimes forever, because this is the feeling that hurts so much and causes us to feel so desperately lonely.

Being strong for this journey is not about how much you can tolerate or avoid, but about how you accept and live through this time. Sorrow can only be endured by being accepted and embraced. When you begin to accept the loss of your marriage as something real, you begin to prepare yourself for the sadness you feel and for the journey through it.

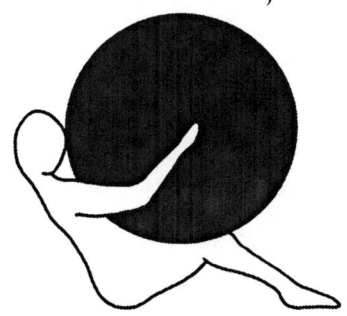

Now might come that divine time, when you begin to convert yourself into a believer of spirituality. Pain often inspires us to do that. You may summon fortune, relearn and recite your prayers, light dozens, and dozens, and dozens of candles, and beg fate on your knees for help. You will implore fervently for another chance for your partner to become who you want and need them to be. *Please make him change.* Call the psychic! Get thee to a drive-in place of worship! Hello God, remember me? False hope will stalk you like the devil, test your courage, and exploit your lack of it, as you instinctively try to avoid the deepest and most personal place on this journey.

Our sadness says who we are in a very deep way. It is created from our losses. The pain of feeling this way touches hard, reminding you better than anything else, of the sober truth about things. It can be hard to let yourself take direction from that now, but if you ignore your pain, it becomes suppressed and manifests itself into depression and disease. This is a nasty soup. You can waste your life in this kind of self-abnegation because by not facing this loss, whether it takes five minutes for you to get it out of your system or five years, you will stay buried in the dark about how you love, and what kind of love you need and desire for yourself. It will remain a tragic, wasted mystery to you and whoever wants to love you. Instead of masquerading around invulnerable now, leave the anger as an enabler for your denial, and allow yourself to be guided by your pain. That is truly where the signs are for you to follow now, believe it or not.

    I could have stayed in a state of anger for the rest of my life. Those facts that enabled me to feel infuriated were going to live and thrive in me forever if I wanted them to. I had such a large cache of them. They would never go away, never stop taunting me as long as I kept them alive and vigorous by feeding them pieces of myself on a daily basis. Feeling angry gave me a purpose, and it gave me something to live for every day. It made me feel important, entitled, and it fueled my energy. It gave me the upper hand. But then, I realized that as long as I harbored anger towards the son of a bitch, I was still keeping myself connected to him. We were still holding hands, and I was afraid to let go. I was afraid to face the truth that my marriage to him had failed and it was all going to be over, never what it once was, not only the bad times that kept us together, but the good times between us would be gone forever as well. To avoid feeling the gnawing pain of my loss and my broken heart, my occupation for the rest of my life was going to be silencing our songs, wiping our special places off the map, burying the movies we saw together, and absolutely forgetting the sweet, wonderful moments that were ours. What was I supposed to do with our daughter in the meantime? Put her in a closet? Send her to boarding school in Switzerland?

I was so busy trying to get away from him, to forget our sad, futile attempts at a life together, that I think I passed over that place where you finally do not care anymore. Does that place even exist outside of anger? I did not know. I would miss him sometimes too, after the dust had settled. I was terrified of having to sift through the ashes and pieces of bone left from the fierce energy that I spent in trying to become strong enough to separate from him. To get to this point, to the fearsome emptiness, to the surrender to separateness, to the disintegration and disunion of us, and to the final split, was so nightmarish an idea that I remained connected to him with the only thing that I had left. I was staying put in my rage.

Perhaps one of those dense, black clouds will park itself over your head for a while. Some people never come away from it. It attaches itself to the psyche and stays there forever, feeding off your negative waves. When this happens, in the midst of living out your sorrow, the clamor of good news could come off as something really oppressive. *Who needs to hear that now?* You may despise it all. *Let them all go to hell.* To avoid any contrast whatsoever to your low spirits, you might lock yourself up in this place of lamenting, where the walls are padded with the facts.

Pardon me, I regret bursting in with news like this, but it is not a bad idea to let yourself be disturbed now. Let a little of the light in, Dracula. In the midst of your miserable-ness, take time to force yourself, and at first you will really have to force yourself, to let in some of the joys of your life. This is the well, the source of your vitality. Know that joy still exists for you, and it could still happen to you, if it hasn't happened already. If you are dying for some light, look at those miracles called your children, your funny and wonderful friends, and the fellow humans in your family who you love for the affection they bestow upon you, and how they make you feel good. Call up your people and ask them to tell you that you matter, and that you are loved and cared about. Tell them that you need to hear it. They will understand if they are your friends. Taking care of yourself and others will become easier then, after accepting some well deserved comfort and care from those you trust.

If I was going to walk around like a zombie, my child might become a zombie too. That was number one. She would be a scared and insecure zombie, the worst kind of zombie you could have. I could not do that to her. She was sweet. She was innocent. Being with her actually afforded me vacation time from my weepy opera. I realized that I didn't need to think so much all of the time. My thoughts about how broken-hearted I was, and my dwelling on the causes of my plight, weighed me down and stopped me from moving; practically stopped me from breathing. I needed to keep going through the necessary motions to keep my life moving. Who said that I had to pay so much attention to my emotional details now? As a matter of fact, the simpler I made my life, the easier it was to live through this time.

Maintain a hold on your everyday needs and tasks, and shed the rest for a time. Make a list if you need to, and perform and check off the things that need to be done. If you work, if you are a parent, if you have responsibilities, the day is over before you know it. Look at the time; you made it through another day…right into your cozy pajamas, with a good book, bed, and sleep. *"Sleep that knits up the ravell'd sleave of care."*

I was a real pill for a good long while too. I still felt the sting of the arrow that pierced through my heart, and I was jealous of all of the stupid, mindless people walking on this earth without pain, giggling and smiling, and appearing light-hearted and happy around me, and everywhere else. *Go jump in the lake already, will you.* Aha! What was that? Envy? Hello envy! I knew from right then and there, that I was still alive and kicking, although you would never know it to look at me…more like death warmed over. Ok, I wanted to live and I wanted to feel happy about it too, as futile as my jealousy of movie stars' lives was, it was a start. I began to use my envy of others in a positive way, as an invitation back into life, rather than fall into the usual resentment and state of vegetation that envy can provoke.

★

When you are emotionally hurt, you project that sadness and depression everywhere in your body. You can feel overcome with waves of unleashed emotion when you are sad and depressed. You become vulnerable to outside forces. You need to take care of yourself when this happens, not take it out on yourself.

You should retreat to the sidelines of this battle, and begin to take refuge into your self. We often just need to let time heal us, but rest as a vacation from living out this time is a great healer too. Going to bed early for a good night's sleep helped me to greet tomorrow with more than just dread. It seems too simple. So many of us, in searching for that thing that makes us feel satisfied and better, have become forgetful of what a good night's sleep feels like. I allowed myself time to read books. What I chose to read confirmed the course I was taking, and where I was going. I took my vitamins. I swam my laps. And I walked. Exercise and good health is an affordable luxury. Seek it out. I sought myself in things that were outside of me, like the creative arts. Embracing the arts can help to heal you because you become aware of the depth of existence, regarded long before you and your marital separation arrived to leave its mark, and history knows a thing or two. Music is good for a broken heart, and it was through my music that I realized my desire to love and to be loved. Leonard Bernstein, the conductor, composer and musician, said that our own feelings are often so deep and confusing, and music can define them. I was all raw needy feeling and was still capable of feeling love, of wanting love. That felt good. And the love for me to accept could come from anywhere. Two minutes of kindness from the grocer could do it for me when I was feeling this vulnerable. At this stage, it was enough.

Sadness was becoming more familiar, and I was feeling more comfortable in this state of mind. From feeling sorry for myself, I developed compassion for kindred spirits who had tragedy and sadness in their lives. Feeling sad every day, and accepting those feelings, is where I found the courage to correct things and locate myself.

Sadness can transform us. It can carry us to another place:

"I believe that almost all our sadnesses are moments of tension that we find paralyzing because we no longer hear our surprised feelings living. Because we are alone with the alien thing that has entered into ourself; because everything that is intimate and accustomed is for an instant taken away; because we stand in the middle of a transition where we cannot remain standing. For this reason the sadness too passes: the new thing in us, the added thing, has entered into our heart, has gone into its inmost chamber and is not even there anymore, - is already in our blood. And we do not learn what it was. We could easily be made to believe that nothing has happened, and yet we have changed, as a home changes into which a guest has entered. We cannot say who has come, perhaps we shall never know, but many signs indicate that the future enters into us in this way in order to transform itself in us long before it happens."

Rainer Maria Rilke, Letters to a Young Poet

When we begin to feel ourselves growing up through our experiences, we begin to understand that one cannot live a life of constant happiness. It is impossible to remain safe and secure in the playpen, with all of our toys and lollipops about, and be an adult at the same time. With no unhappiness and sacrifice in our lives, we cannot grow. We cannot evolve, become wise and help others to grow. We stay the same always, and now in this day and age when it is so easy and desirable to look the same always, it is tempting to reside in our heads in what we are afraid to admit is really a state of stagnation.

Sometimes, when we finally do move into a state of sadness and begin to mourn, we start to worry about having to lose our sorrow before we are ready. After all, this is a kind of holding on, even though it is the bitter end. It's better than nothing. People tell us to cheer up, and the always impatient world wants us to keep moving, keep moving. They want to sell us magic pills and procedures that will wipe out all of our fears and worries, and send us through the factory repair remade and reprogrammed and not giving a damn anymore.

Know that your feelings are yours. You own them. They are precious and human. No one can tell you how to feel or how long to feel that way. It is our right to be tormented by our wretchedness for as long as we want to be. Getting away from the grieving for a while just keeps your life more in balance, and keeps the ball rolling when it has to. When you need to return to your crying, your sadness will be there, waiting for you, holding up your widow's weeds for you to don, for you to continue. You will eventually emerge through your heartache, and finally let it go when you are ready.

If you find that you are not moving through this time as well as you want to and need to be, and you feel lost in depression, good honest therapy is a device that can guide you to where you want to go safely, through to the next place. We take our shoes to the shoemaker, so sometimes we need to take our racked-out, tired minds to someone who can help us sort things out and see beyond our woes. Seeking out therapy for the more difficult times in your life is a healthy and courageous response to something that continues to bring you down.

My therapist, who was not the first one who I met with but the one that I chose, showed me how to carry my burdens more effectively, and she was unobjectionable when the time came when I felt I could carry on by myself again. She was a therapist who helped me to grow through my crisis. She was there for me; I wasn't there for her. She listened to me, with all of her books on the shelf behind her, while sitting confidently in her chair, and I felt like she cared about me. She talked to me and gave me insight into myself. She held the lantern through the dark tunnel for me while she gave objective, sound advice on how to proceed. She was available to me on the telephone if I needed to speak to her. I could have sought out a male therapist for my cause, or anyone who qualified to help me. The Easter Bunny could have had the job if it would have worked out that way. Help came to me because I was ready to seek it out, to trust the advice as long as I was telling the truth, and accept it and do my homework. It came from the correct places because I never gave up on trusting my instincts and believing in myself.

✶

As women, we know the tragedies and dramas, and we have been taught and trained to play them. We have all witnessed and identified with the passions and failures of female characters who don't make it, go insane, become abandoned, homeless, alcoholic or drug-addicted, labeled as sluts, loose their children, commit suicide or be murdered, turn bitter, angry, ugly, poor, sick, become old maids and end up and die alone. It is no wonder that it is so hard for us to separate into ourselves. Look at all those tragic endings we have been shown to fear on a daily basis if we do.

I was still feeling really depressed every day, and it seemed like it would never end. Every day, day after day, I lugged and dragged about the same weighted-down, pent-up feelings. I drew my energy from feeling like a failure. I feared that my life was over, but that was okay because so far it was a miss-lived life, full of mistakes, and mistaken identities and all sorts of negativity like that. What a fool! Like my living in a state of anger, living a crappy life seemed to become a part of my job now too. *The violins come in now, fortissimo.* One day I couldn't stand to feel this way anymore. It was enough of a punishment to feel this building up of my emotions each day with no release whatsoever.

I was faced head on with the moment of having to let go of my resistance to really feeling my anguish about what was true, and get it over with. I had to finally answer the doorbell to this pest at my door, and swallow the bitter pill of his power over me. I had to admit that the glass slipper did not fit anymore; that this was my midnight. My nervous anticipation, as if I was to have root canal tomorrow sans anesthetic, of what it would feel like if I really let it all touch me, all at once, if I just let it all in, kept postponing my acceptance of my deepest feelings. But one day, like a child who has been stung by a bee, I hollered ouch without reservation, and at the top of my lungs I screamed out his name. Jeffrey! Then I finally started to cry.

"I wept not, so to stone within I grew."
Dante Alighieri, Italian poet

Dante's words deserve pride of place on my paper. Don't be afraid to cry. It's not so bad. It can feel good to release it. Crying can be a way for you to let go of deep, heartfelt, feelings that hurt. I wished that I had cried forty years ago. To avoid taking that plunge into suffering the most difficult feelings of disappointment, loss, despair, fear and mourning is to avoid moving forward on this journey. By this time in your life, you might have expected deep, rich, well-established feelings inside of your heart about your partner and your marriage. The keepsake trunk in the attic has been opened and with shock and surprise you find inside, not the anticipated treasures of long-awaited hopes and fantasies come to life, but moth-eaten, shattered dreams.

Crying releases the sadness from within your heart. These feelings of sadness are noble. They say who you are. When you cry, you get closer to your true self, even though at the same time you must let go of something that you may not be ready to part from yet. When you connect with your pain, you accept your feelings. If other people are causing your pain, you have the option of telling them how you feel. You can declare yourself to you, and to others if you want to, and in this way you can move forward on your own. This is the way to forgiveness.

When you allow yourself to express feelings of pain openly to yourself and to the ones that cause it, you can finally start to release that pain. Let go of it. You will finally be able to crack through that weeping image of sorrow and cosmic gloaming that you thought would never end, and emerge as someone who remembers the pain, but who can now be interested in the adventure, and in the future. This is the way to freedom.

If facing and accepting our sadness bestows upon us courage, and moving through it definitely makes us stronger, we might begin to treat our partners and anyone else who has hurt us like dirt. We may blame them for causing our sadness, and fall back into our anger and want to burn their house down. This can be a sign of progress to most of us who were afraid to react in any way to anyone's negative effect on us. We still want people to change.

It takes more courage to stop denigrating others. It means that you can take responsibility for your own feelings. It means that you have the guts to accept things for what they are and may always be, whether you like it or not. You can honestly admit to understanding that things are outside of your control, and yet, you can still carry on. Separating from someone emotionally that way takes much more self-confidence and survivability, than setting up camp in their aura and despising them.

Sadness and mourning is one thing, but if you fall back into the trap of asking questions about your self-worth and why was I born because of the way someone is behaving or treating you, it is time to revisit what you learned from a state of rational, and focused anger, or go back to therapy to enable you to climb out of that state of self-loathing. You have come so far, away from so much of it. Why turn back now?

Unfortunately, our sadness will not transform the other guy. It transforms us. Change from the role of the victim to the role of observer. You were born and you are still alive. Don't waste this time. Look around you and be thankful that you are leaving what you cannot stand anymore. Change the torments to affirmations now. You have won the battle if you have come this far.

If you have cried your heart out and then some, you have earned the right to move on from this time, and you will find the strength to do so from accepting the truth about things, and by not being afraid to live with the knowledge of it. You emerge out of your misery with wounds, but they are going to heal. All of what you have been through up to now will call you back for a new challenge, time and time again, but it is a familiar ground. You know the route. Are you damaged goods now? That depends on your attitude. In moments of recurring shame and self-pity, that definition works well to send us to a place of retreating into ourselves, to get back to the real us that we have forgotten again.

At the same time, a feeling of triumph on the horizon is something new, and an alternative feeling that we might not be used to or know what to do about. Some of us have never come close to such a feeling, except in the movies, and other untouchable circumstances that are beyond our scope and reality. We are conditioned to feeling far removed from such a selfish emotion anyway, even though we admire it from afar. It is such an unfamiliar terrain. Yet, it is in our territory.

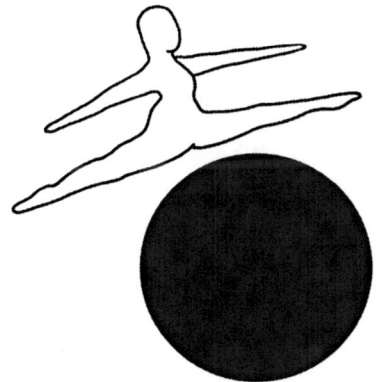

The Coming of the Light

"If I've only one life, let me live it as a blonde!"
Miss Clairol ad campaign slogan

Now what? There is illumination from over here as opposed to no illumination from over there. Here is the bridge to your light as a result of your reflections. Say welcome to your island.

After the yelling and screaming, the crying and more crying, and all the madness and the fury, it was time for a healing. At this point I really needed to glue my bones back together. My future, still uncertain, became even more of a concern and at times a real worry, but I still felt entitled to being on this journey because I saw it as a new beginning for me. How long will your luck hold out? When you go through emotional turmoil but try to see more outside of it, you are more likely to land in the right place. Although you may feel that you are being buried alive, you will eventually emerge wiser and with more insight. You need to remember that experience is a passage. Unless you are in some sort of a state of walking unconsciousness, you have to learn something from all that has occurred to you. Something has to click somewhere.

It is important to remember that you are separating from a very strong connection. After you begin to take this fact into consideration, you will think it astounding that more people in similar situations do not realize this. If they did, they would seek more insight and make it their priority to understand this process better. They would be more determined to move forward through this change in the most positive way, rather than staying stuck in the mud. Regardless of how hard it is to admit to fears of facing the future separated, this is not the end of the world. This is your journey through marital separation to a new world.

To finally accept the facts of what has defined itself as pretty certain, after a time of numerous rude awakenings, can be liberating. You are freed from the excruciating wonder. You can stop drowning now and learn to swim. Although there is a partner out there who affects us, it is we who must selfishly decide our fate. How dare you? Well, you should advertise to the world that you have emerged from out of the darkness and maybe the world will receive your message. Here you are. You realize why you did some things. You realize why you felt the way you felt. You did not perish and go to hell. You grew from it. Change can indeed be positive. I felt strangely expanded as if I was going up like a vine. For my first step into the limelight, the cosmetics industry was waiting for my re-arrival, as only they know how to do.

I had been trudging for so long on this particularly difficult journey, that now was the time for me to find my oasis and become a fashion victim. If you want to change or improve your physical appearance now, to declare the new you to the world and to yourself, do it. This is a fanfaronade for the return of your energy and the rebirth of your self-confidence. This is healthy vanity filling up the long lost empty spaces inside of you. Allow yourself to look the way you want to look now. If anyone tells you that you don't look like you anymore, consider it a compliment. With renewal there is surprise.

In this place, you can find yourself perplexed by a new ambience, even though it is you who have changed your course and started the process of ending up here. You might harbor shame and embarrassment about a sudden new burst of forgotten energy that feels like you are saying f - you to the world. You might begin to sneak a peek at the new you, who feels no longer inferior to everything, in spite of how difficult it can be to put that into practice in your life. Are your shoes on the wrong feet? Who cares?

Look in the mirror. This is the other person that you might have secretly wanted to be for some time. It scares you to look at her because she haunts you now, and will continue to haunt you until you accept her. What a contrast you have become to a world that is suddenly outside of you. You have indeed changed, grown, and moved to a different place by now. Not backwards in time, because as you have probably discovered, this experience changes you and pushes you on. This becomes apparent when you discover how your experience with the outside world has changed, and how what you have experienced so far has reinvented you. You are more separate now than you ever were and more connected to yourself. After the first shock of this, you sing out loud with the most optimistic of voices. Do not feel guilty about feeling better. This is what you wanted all along. There is no other positive way to feel now, even though you still feel the loss brought on by this change, welcomed or otherwise.

I wanted to sing and dance but I was afraid that the floor would cave in. I pretended that I wasn't being naive. That feeling, like I have emerged from battle intact, should have left me more serious and more grown up. Why did I only want to go shopping? This is so superficial, I kept saying to myself.

Be more sober. How foolish will I look now as I attempt to apply my new let's have a party attitude, which might have seemed much too frivolous and too pompous at the time, across to the world? At least let's go to dinner.

When you are separating into yourself, sometimes the most challenging part of the process is when you emerge from your deep spiritual and emotional concerns, and your immediate priorities level off to the superficial, if only for a time. There seems to be so little to hold on to when this happens because we judge ourselves by what we involve ourselves with. We feel more significant when we are holding on to something heavy and deep, struggling not to drop it. This behavior pleases others more than us, and we fall under the illusion that we will be kept safe in this new place as long as we are penitent. Nonsense. Here is an ideal time for a much-needed opportunity to rest and take a break from the struggling and gasping for breath. This is a time to pause, rest, refuel, and reflect on things now, while you feel tanked up rather than diminished. Now is a good time to find more insight into what and why things happened from this new point of view. It might matter a great deal to you that you came out of your battle alive, even awarded with a new lease on life, but what will it matter to anyone else, especially as you naturally act out your survival in public? This is a good time to practice acceptance of the fact that you cannot control people's thoughts about you. Your insecurities are telling you that you are selfishly giving yourself a needless parade. Who else really cares about all that you have been through and emerged from besides your mother?

How could you be less self-conscious now? You have managed to clear a path from the idea of being a separate person to actually beginning to live as a separate you in the world. As you move on through this phase, it is a new day and you might change something about yourself physically so you can establish this new beginning. It feels strange to show any optimism or even a new pair of high heels. Yet most of us cannot just sit and examine our lives like Socrates, or become nun-like and retreat to a convent, or worry all the time under an aura of invisibility in lieu of lying on a bed of nails. Most of us just want to get our hair and nails done now. Maybe even throw in a facial. We no longer feel that we have to look good or bad for our partners, as much as we feel the need to look like and be ourselves. No one else really has to see us because we can see ourselves, and the visuals emerge strong here. Even though you may still find yourself a poor excuse for survival, the need to make an attempt at it is here. As awkward as a new beginning for ourselves feels, we need to try it out in the best way that we know how, and accept the fact that we feel entitled to grow into this change in our own way, which unfortunately, in this case, is up, up and away.

★

Separating into yourself spares you the necessity of having to please others all of the time. From this vantage point, you enter into the self-confidence you attain from just being you, and you should feel relieved of some of the guilt and panic that you might feel, or are used to feeling, when you don't please others every single second of your life. There is the disheartening discovery of those who have pretty much done very little for you in life except bring you down, and up to now you may have worried about disappointing them. You might have known about them all along because you took their blows, but this is the time that you take it in because you are ready to feel it now. You are no longer afraid to. You want to react to it now in a brand new way also, but you don't have to. Fall back on the fact of you. You have your own power and you are in control. Isn't that a scary notion? You have the power now to say no and mean it. You own the power to refuse to bite the carrot that is hung in front of your nose. You can turn the other cheek. You do not have to get involved in it another minute longer because you own the power to walk away. You earn this place when you refuse to give your energy and thoughts to it. You earn this place when you begin to set boundaries.

You know the way you want to look, and live, and grow now, regardless of how much money you have or don't have, how much weight you have gained or lost, what kind of car you drive or if you even have one at all, and how much stuff that you have or don't have in comparison to others. It is truly about who you are now and not about what you have, or whom you have to please or impress. As you begin to feel some freedom from the pressure of the wrong sensibilities, you will be able to hear advice now, even from the best intentioned, without feeling the pressure of having to obey. It feels like less and less that anyone has any power over you at all. You can listen without resentment now and decide for yourself.

Suddenly there are doors. There are doors for you to enter and doors for you to close. These are new options presenting themselves to you as a result of your passage. A long hallway of Alice in Wonderland like doors presented itself to me and I never felt so much freedom to choose before. The most gratifying thing for me was to close some doors. The most frightening yet exciting thing was to open doors, even the ones that led to the extreme unknown, or the ones that I had to slam shut immediately upon looking in. I wasn't going in there again! The wisest thing I could do now was to wait for more direction and information before I walked through any doors at all.

Wanting and needing desperately to discover new opportunities, after some very hard, emotionally lean years, resulted in states of impatience and frustration for me. I wanted and needed new things that were right for me now. Wasn't it about time, I thought? I was ready. I had waited so long. I wasn't getting any younger, either. I wanted it to happen now. I looked pretty good now too, from all those visits to the beauty parlor. But I really was not ready. My unrequited dreams and desires were dictating deadlines to me.

New insecurities emerge now. What you have learned about yourself up to now is great and valuable, but you must have patience to accept the pace of this journey and not be tempted to act prematurely out of desperation and fear. You can console yourself while anxiously waiting for some of your needs to be met, by knowing that you have tried and succeeded each and every day to prove yourself capable of moving forward and making the right choices, and you did. You will continue to reap what you sow if you keep going the way that you have been. The best thing now is to relish the fact that you possess the power to choose any new opportunities that come your way. The greatest thing is that you find the strength and the desire to pursue these opportunities based on your own set of values, not everybody else's.

Sometimes, when we do begin to emit rays of our survivability and our renewed capacity for life, we are presented with new chances before we are emotionally ready. Be careful what you wish for. It may come at your beck and call. This can cause the ultimate state of confusion and a sense of harking back, homesickness, and nostalgia. How about a little soul-searching to get back to you? Remember that you are on a mission to improve your life. Take the time to get back into your brain and think, and become clear-headed about what are your fears and trepidations. These are your road signs now. Pay attention to them. Anything that is worthwhile, or anyone who is, will give you adequate time to make a decision, whether you want to go with it or not. If you feel a sense of desperation and a fear of another loss, especially another loss of yourself, then you know that this is not something to attach yourself to. Say thank you very much and keep separate from what might be forcing you back into a repeat scenario.

Always trust your gut. You can come to a decision about anything in secret and live with it for a few hours, or for a day, or even for years before you decide what to do. How do you feel? What are you leaving behind and what will you gain? If you have children, your happiness means their happiness. There should be no compromises now for them. Based on this, it should be easy to keep moving forward on your mission, even if you have to move forward quicker than you thought, and suddenly leave your past faster than you wished or thought yourself capable of.

You are going to find out now who are your real friends and who are not. It can be a letdown and a surprise. The outside world and its possibilities may lose some of the verve and possibility that it held for you when you were younger, before your marriage, when you felt an optimistic anticipation of your future. It seems like there is less to hold on to now as you walk around in this time both of new beginnings and also of endings, cursing your hard earned wisdom, with many of your familiar things seemingly turning to liquid. Some of your attachments with old, out-dated lifestyles and relationships will start to come to a close. Sing *Auld Lang Syne*, and believe that you will have better, more meaningful ones as you grow through this major event in your life. Feel this especially for your children if you have any. Your hope and faith in change for a better future will transfer over to them, and they will need that as a source from you now. New priorities emerge and this is a time to recognize and embrace them.

This is a good time to practice letting go. Now that you feel a little life coming back into you and the promise of hope returning, use this time to get rid of stuff. While some of your focus is on the material, allow the sentiment from the hundreds of things that you have accumulated because you were afraid to throw them out or give them away enter your heart. Ok, it is there; now let it go. Good. Believe in the power of memory. If it is in your heart, it will never leave you. You have yourself now. The need to hoard all sorts of things is over because what is that all about anyway? Some of those things that you thought that you could never part with will not bring about what you missed out on in life anyway. In fact, they keep you connected and bound to the same old neediness and unfulfilled desires. This is a time to dare to feel refreshed and revived, and a little lighter in load. Are you moving? This can be a good excuse to fool your mind into letting things go with a practical purpose, although your true purpose is to free up your mind to focus on what really matters.

Do not be wary of a vacant shelf or bureau drawer. The anticipation of what will eventually be placed there can be yet another exercise in self-discovery, self-improvement, and hope. Be fussy and particular. Learn to wait. Trust in what may be out there for you but not here yet. Do not give in to the fear of not having a lot right now. Be curious first and embrace the emptiness now. If you cannot let go of the same old things, you will continue to live with your old clutter in your old life. This means that your emotional clutter will follow you as well. Will you feel regret? Not for long, when the lightness that you feel lifts you up and you cease to identify with the old gravity that keeps you down. Not from pilled, outdated sweaters and dusty old knickknacks that have gone from your life, out of fashion and into the bin, but from people who feel abandoned by you will you notice some resentment. It may smart to hear them tell you about it and weaken you when they press you on it. Just stay on your path and keep growing.

✶

When you begin to light your own fire, you ignite your courage to stand back and observe yourself and others. You might see that your life was led into error more than you thought it was. It is easier to admit to failure now, and the forgiveness of yourself and others helps you to be more open and receptive, and not as alone as you thought you were. When you start to embrace life as an experience that you have control over, you draw to you a life that is lived in a new way. Even if it feels like it is taking endless amounts of energy and time to find your way through this change, you should ask yourself "where am I going in the meantime?" Is there another route that you should be taking now? You will find the answer to what the rush is all about and where you should be going when you see your life realistically day to day, rather than in a blur of futuristic wonder and maniacal approach.

Now that you feel stronger, less needy, and more separate, thoughts of acting out from a need for revenge dissipate, and you are finally relieved of this cumbersome burden. You can discover that connections and interactions do not always have to end with violence. This new attitude towards a way of looking back to the past, and today to the present, helps you to move forward on your journey with more trust and confidence, and you will have less to worry about because you will not have to be moved to charging and attacking behavior every time you need to work something out. It is a small victory that you can feel in a big way. Because you can start to trust yourself and feel less vulnerable, you can allow any behavior of others help you to affirm yourself as separate, as you walk away and begin to get to know your own ideas for the future.

Kindness brings strength for being separate and it is a much better alternative to retribution and spite, which actually is another way to stay connected. Let the good stuff sprout. Humanity knows no shame. Compassion is a perfect vehicle to drive away the anger and depression you feel at being manipulated, retroactively or otherwise. Your empathy towards others can help you to release any fear that you will lose your separateness in the wake of their behavior towards you. With the power of kindness and compassion, the ugly stuff goes out the window. Ungrudging and charitable thoughts, even though practicing this at first may feel like your head is in a vice grip, makes you a better person and you will feel the results from it. Guilt about whom and what you want to leave behind evaporates in the knowing that you can love and care about the people who deserve it, and you will feel no longer entrapped by others unwillingly. The power of benevolence through understanding can help you to hold the upper hand and help you to set limits and boundaries in the midst of bad behavior. It gives you the power to stay in your own world without worrying about being sucked into someone else's.

When you stop thinking of yourself as a victim, for the sake of your life and your fate, you become active rather than anxious, and refuse to return to a past unpleasant. You stop demanding the attention for a poor hurt soul, and feel surprised to draw a different attention that credits you with being you. You can look back and reflect, rather than fight back at everything, and move ahead on your journey now with what you need to change your life.

I got through the worst of it because here I was, still standing, having come from a place where I was scared out of my wits, confused, always feeling like the only one, driven to temporary insanity, and finally touched and moved to tears, but still intact. How did that happen? It must have been a miracle. Yet this difficult and arduous emotional topography would come back to challenge me again, and become even more intense and disorganized because my journey was not over. The strongest emotions would haunt me at three in the morning, be exorcised by the sunrise with the sound of a bird singing somewhere, and curiously return to be refigured, with my resolve strengthened, and hopefully be confirmed later on. What I found once repellent became interesting when I could take myself out of it and observe. But this took a great deal of work and willpower, and many of those sleepless nights, to trust myself enough to leave so much of my old unhappy life, and so much of what I once loved and still loved, behind.

Once you might have been compelled to dictate every move of your passage to others, even just for the company. This can be a very lonely journey, and few of us like to travel alone. Your telephone might have been busy for hours with the details of your every step. What happens now, with more occurring inside of you, and with you taking possession of more of yourself and less of others and their reactions, is that there is more that you want to keep to yourself. You realize that your story is special, and you do not have to search for affirmations outside of you now. You discover the meaning of privacy. You will also see that with time, everyone will have forgotten about your dilemma and will seek out fresh news. Since you have stopped feeding them your tidbits, they have moved to another snack bar.

Your life is becoming yours. If you are thinking of changing the color of your hair, a new beginning has to start somewhere. As a blonde, a brunette, or a redhead, you will realize down the road that it really doesn't matter what color it is, so go for it.

Entrapments, Delays, and Stops

"The most valuable men aboard a fishing boat are those who can successfully wear the blinders, who can see the light at the end of the tunnel, no matter how dim, and who can be most imaginative when dealing with the obstacles that threaten to pull the shade."

Linda Greenlaw, swordboat captain, The Hungry Ocean

Fears and difficulties that you might have successfully worked through within the safe cocoon of familiar relationships, such as connections with your partner, your family and your friends, emerge now from a place of the unknown. The impact of some of these effects coming towards you from the outside world can feel overpowering and compelling.

You may feel relieved at this point to have finally let go of and separated from some of the burdens of others; burdens that you were shouldering even though they were never yours to carry in the first place. Expect to carry your own burdens of responsibility now, as your journey continues through to your new life. Although here is a much heavier weight to bear, it is yours and worth the weight. The first thing that you must do to carry on is to stop blaming others, so that you can see through to the strength and direction that is within you to move on. Blaming it all on the outside only keeps us stuck in the place we so desperately want to move away from.

This can be the place where you stop to realize where you are, say yikes, loose your nerve, and decide to return to the safety of your past life, if only to let go of all of the stress and worry that you have to carry now all by yourself. It is tempting to turn back amongst the headwinds, and only human to want to. You know that your past will accept your return with open arms, and then, like before, you will know what to expect from tomorrow. Even if it means spending your life with something that you no longer possess, living with the familiar and knowing what to expect from even your hardest trials is a comforting and persuasive concession. As you look back from where you are now, standing alone and vulnerable in what appears as a bleak and forbidding wilderness, you might think back on a life that seemed easy then and alluringly innocent, even if you were depressed for most of the time. Now here you are, estranged by your own doing from a place you could at least call home. Suddenly finding yourself in a new place and living with less than what you are used to, emotionally and physically, may challenge your faith in yourself, and in your decision to separate from what was at least comfortably familiar.

To keep steady on your way and to retain equilibrium, it is important to understand that a new life does not suddenly fall into place by a simple turn of a key or click of a switch. A new life takes time to unfold. What you fill each day with will determine the outcome of your journey. Instead of losing out to a negative outlook for what seems like a distant and unattainable new start, live in the here and now, and use this time as a classroom, to learn and to grow towards what you are seeking, step by step.

My husband would not move in all sorts of ways, so it was up to me to flee if I really wanted to. This undertaking, including the emotional leaving that I took upon myself to initiate big time, compounded everything into one big unfortunate state of affairs. Thankfully, the searching for living space of my own felt relieving, with the promise of clean air, peace and renewal, and a change of walls. All the possibilities of charm and convenience, and a new life materialized within ten minutes of walking through an empty space of potential for me. I'll take it!

When moving day came, I was brought to my knees by the force and impact of my decision, which would completely eclipse this marriage pronto. There, with the harsh realness of moving men who couldn't give a damn, my belongings and my daughter's toys bidding farewell in cardboard boxes, and my furniture being carted out to who knows where, a cruel picture of what I expected to be my triumph at last, floored me. My ashen-faced husband suddenly caught my pity when I had been despising him and depriving him of a connection with me for years. Everything I had worked so hard for and believed in my heart for my daughter and me seemed to have betrayed us as soon as it became real.

Alone that night in the tiny living room, with too much of my furniture piled up all around me, with no feasible place to put it, I had nothing to do but be stunned by what had just taken place. My daughter cried herself to sleep in her strange new room without Daddy, and I was so numb and exhausted from what felt like the worst day of my life that I could not comfort her. I thought of my husband and how it must have been for him to be alone at our deserted apartment, especially without being able to check on his daughter tonight sleeping peacefully in her bed. How strong does a family have to be to live through this kind of a day? This was the heart wrenching parting at the station, the urgent blowing of the whistle, and the train was pulling out before we all had a chance to say goodbye.

Here was a grim vacancy where I would have to live until time and my actions helped fill up my life again. During the most dreadful moments of life, you need to draw from a source of hope each day, rather than draw from future's well by fishing for sure answers for tomorrow. The assurances and solutions that we demand from the future now, to make our anxieties easier to bear today, take us off our path. We could possibly find ourselves in places of future's promise, but with the answers to our questions still unlived, and before we know it, we are too old, without having ever attained the faith, perseverance, and confidence to grant our wishes ourselves. The wellspring that carries hopefulness is right where you are now, even if it feels like you are nowhere.

Before I knew it, the train was pulling into the station again, but this time it came barreling through for real, as a commuter train, directly under the windows of my new apartment. I had not realized this thunderous passing at precisely the same time each day, except on weekends and holidays, would be so intense. When I took the apartment, I was aware that the tracks were down there somewhere, but I never realized that the noise from the trains could be so loud. Those trains passed through my life so ridiculously loud and shook everything so disarmingly that it became a laughable calamity after I took it as a good omen. I was on my way! Do not ever lose your sense of humor.

You could find yourself terribly alone with the world's punishing reactions when you struggle on the high seas through the darkness of change. Sometimes it is difficult to find the lessons, no matter how level headed and sane you try to remain, and no matter how hard you look. For instance, there were these upstairs neighbors who were horribly noisy and cruelly dismissive to my pleas of "please, I have a young child who has to get up for school in the morning." A cockroach escaped behind the kitchen counter at two in the morning. The super of my new building began making it very apparent that he didn't like me. Like a huge wave, unfamiliarity washed over me and soaked me in despair. Disappointment took the place of hopes for the better, and I became frozen in a cold and barren land. As a woman alone with a young child, I was fated by a two-year lease in a place with no history for me to draw on, and from here it seemed that there was very little assurance that the direction I was heading was the right one.

When this happens, it helps to let your thoughts revisit a good time in your past for strength to cope with the vagueness of the present. Perhaps you had a pleasant childhood that you can reflect on. Supportive parents, family and friends can remind us of the fact that our life extends out from our predicaments, and they can be there in many different ways to help us to carry on. The things that my parents gave me, large things and the tiniest things, good and bad, and the values and lessons that I learned and took with me from being their child helped me to keep going in spite of it all. Who I am as a result helped me to keep going. Even the bad, unpleasant things from your past, the things that occurred that you would prefer to wipe out of your mind forever can help you now. This is the time to bring them all out of the vault. Finally they are of good use to you. See, you never know. Use these experiences, these feelings that you prefer to keep buried, to your advantage now. Use the data of your entire lifetime up to now to get you through this. It has all been worthwhile for the things that it teaches you now.

✳

You thankfully discover that the cancer you suspected is an allergy, but you still run aground from the fear of losing all that you have gained so far. Your resistance to the happiness within you is disabling your desires. You might be harboring some repressed anger or guilt towards others and yourself for allowing this change to occur. Letting go of the reliability of negativity and reaching for the far-fetched idea of contentment can be a pretty frightening thing to do when there are no guarantees.

Fear is the source of all negative emotions. It keeps life's gifts away. Fear of illness and death, fear of the unknown, fear that you are not worthy, fear that you cannot protect yourself from the outside world blocks energy from flowing and blocks you from knowing and taking it in. A clear mind released from negative energy opens the way for positive energy to flow freely. Fear of tomorrow can be overwhelming. On this journey, fear of today upon wakening to its alarm can be simply paralyzing and make you want to go right back into the bed.

You have come so far through the darkness. What if you fail? What was all that work for? Well then, fail. Fail beyond praise because you were doing something for you. Fail on your own terms and on your own turf. It is better to fail at being you than to never have tried. All that is done for the sake of you is never lost.

I felt very alone and isolated in the world. And yet, I had to be the world for my young daughter, who was dependent on me and needed a sound-minded, rational mom, especially now. All of a sudden, people's impressions of me as a strong brave woman were wrong. This did not fit who I felt I really was. I was supposed to emerge as a better me with a better life, and I was supposed to look and feel happier. That is why I took this descent into hell. What happened to the coming of the light? I felt diminished and I identified with an ant. Then, in glowing neon, there it was, a horrendous, blinking, glowing sign, bright as the sun, and lighting up my sorry horizon with a great big fat ugly arrow pointing backwards: This Way, and spelling out the words: **Maybe you should not have left.**

    We are used to living in a world where we believe anger, deception, guilt, and afflictions, and living and breathing in those manifestations over and over again, are the only things that are real and dependable. This has become the norm that keeps us certain. The whole idea of love and love's manifestations has become nothing more than a vaporous fantasy played out on television, and it does not support us as well as hatred does. Love has lost its meaning. If we cannot buy love, screw it, kill it and devour it, fill it up with gas and drive it, flaunt it, and wear it and take it home to add to the rest of our many possessions, it eludes us. We end up living our lives defensively in the real love that we do manage and are lucky enough to attain for ourselves because we fear that it can be stolen from us at any time. We give it no weight. We allow our love and joy to be taken by any small puny thief who wants to rip it off and twist it around himself. We will even hand it over gladly because we have lost the all-out conception of love.

The power of fear on this passage is strong. Hiding in the shadows of your future is a nerve-racking, sinister monster, licking its chops and beckoning you forward for the rest of your life to enter its sad ending realm of doom. Accidents, illnesses and unfortunate experiences can seep in through any weaknesses that we leave open and vulnerable at this time of self-doubt and worry. They sit and wait on the side of the road, like angry ex-in-laws, until you hit a pothole. I have and still do encounter unrelenting beckoning from my past, the stuff that I fought so hard to let go of and leave. I have to fight almost every day to stay separate from it still. Family with their same old dusty routines, the-ex husband (need I say more?), old acquaintances who pop up now and then to tell me that they are still not dead, in fact, they haven't changed a bit, everyone in the world's unleashed insecurities, and intimidating predators who blow themselves up in my face to get my attention, just seem to never go away. And they probably never will.

It all happens everyday right in front of our eyes. Why not want to get away from it, in spite of the untold that we cannot see? Why not look past it all to seek the light ahead? My future, even when I mark it with the stamp of the terrifying unknown, is still my light ahead. Unlike my past and the things that I hate, it stays out there in the waiting room, as a constant and patient possibility, until I am ready to call it in, approach it, and greet it.

✷

If you cannot separate from your old unwanted agendas, you will continue to attract the same people and experiences as you did before. They will find you and recognize you from the signals you put out. You must work, and work, and work until there is no emotional connection to the negative aspects of those people anymore. To attract a different experience with anyone, you must change what you project towards others and the outside world. The future is your own invention when you take responsibility for your actions.

When you embark on a passage to self-discovery, new people and situations feel unfamiliar and can cause you to feel out of place and uncomfortable. Relax. Pull yourself out of the situation, and listen and observe what is going on around you. You do not have to act all the time now, and you possess the power to do nothing or walk away. When you finally get to a place of yourself, you can be in impossible situations and still hold your own until it's time to go home. You need time to get used to a new terrain. For so long, you clung to a certain ground and your tracks on that path made some very deep impressions. It can take time to climb out of those old, well-trodden footprints and onto a new unexplored land.

Once the burden of having to react to everything is let go, life can become much lighter and easier to bear. Take the time to remember your true purpose. If the car breaks down, it is only a car. If your child spills milk, it is an accident. Your child is probably more affected than you are about it. Help them through it rather than use it as another thing to be upset about. If someone cruelly dismisses you or screams at you in rage, for whatever reason, that's his problem, isn't it? One of the ways we can move forward positively and with more confidence in spite of all of it, is by making sure we do not continue to attach ourselves to people and events that make us feel weak and afraid, or try to drag us into their angry slum of a life.

There is much mean-spirited aggression in the world and everyone feels entitled to working his or hers out. This could happen upon you as a surprise, if you were thinking that the world would improve when you do. Just because you are a nice person, do not fall under the false impression that your kindness is contagious. Some people are immune to kindness. *Just because you were able to save yourself from one jerk doesn't mean that there aren't any more jerks out there.* We can return to a sort of naiveté after our rebirth, but we must also grow wise enough to remind ourselves where we came from and what we left behind.

Don't let the facts of it all get you down. Learn the lesson again to break the connection from what does not feel right to you. So what if you need to learn *yet again*. You are probably getting smarter and smarter. Under no circumstances should you join in the madness. Be separate from it and if you are still interested, analyze it later. Believe that protecting yourself and your family from negativism is a priority, and it will become much easier to remove yourself from all of it eventually, even though it will always be around you, waiting for you to let it in. It has nothing else to do.

From a need to announce the new you to the world, or by just practicing your reentrance to yourself, you might meet up with friction that you did not expect, and this could be as a reaction against who you are trying too hard to become. It took time and some hard labor for me to learn that most valuable lesson, that I was better off most of the time if I kept my mouth shut, and stopped overreacting to this change. It was time to remove my medals and trophies that I wore and carried around for all to see. I was not an authority yet. But, I was in combat mode; I had to show my new found guts. In trying so zealously and desperately to control my life so to keep the evil spirits away, I was way outside of my space. I was becoming the new traffic commissioner, fashion police, sanitation inspector, amateur marriage counselor, hurter of feelings for my own benefit, and a constant bloody bore. I went back to my home and back to my personal environment for grounding. I needed to learn to become more humble, and I needed to learn that, in this case, a silent woman is all right as long as she still thinks. The all over the place behavior was all over for me because this was not who I wanted to become. I saw that the difficulties I felt were against me actually guided me to a better place; a place that I would never reach on my own without these challenges. The lesson for me to learn was not to become hardened and militant in response to what had happened to me. The lesson for all of us is to take in the facts, and say thank you to the people who kick us in the teeth, especially when we need that reaction to help us to find our own way again.

We hide our heads in the sand, like those ostriches in cartoons do, when we see our children going through this change with us. We forget sometimes that they are living beings emotionally attached to us, justifiably linked to our every word and move. Where do we expect them to harbor feelings if not with us? Would we prefer for them to take to heart outside on the street somewhere, or in someone else's home? Your children are with you on this journey. They need you as a parent more than ever now. You cannot spare them this experience. You cannot deposit children into your life, then only bring them out and awaken them when the occasion rises. It is distressing that they have to have this experience, but tragic if they cannot get through it. Setting the right examples, guiding and unselfishly teaching your children how to live through this change can allow you to accept your own childhood experiences, and everyone can move on.

I was fragile: handle with care. I needed parenting, damn it. My needy, I want my mommy state of mind was often interrupted by events that reminded me that I was the parent now, such as when I would be talking to my therapist on the telephone and my daughter would be yelling from her bath, "I need a cup! I need a cup!" Dinner still needed to be cooked, and what might that be tonight, you ask? Her homework had to be checked. Do it over. Again. Lunch would need to be prepared at 7 am, packed up, and ready to go, on every single school day. It seemed like invitations to those Saturday morning birthday parties never ceased, and they were held in places where I would have rather died than go. There was the need to keep enough money in the checking account, and then some for emergencies, and then there was the making sure for weeks that she was rid of the head lice that she caught during her first month in kindergarten. I would weigh out all of the urgent needs and the current events and hers always won. But guess what? My reward for letting her win, in the short run, was that I was always so exhausted at the end of each day that I slept like a rock at night. There was no energy left, even to think. My reward in the long run, and still bringing in returns, is watching her grow up into a happy, secure child who feels loved and nurtured adequately.

If you are out on your own and there is not as much money as you used to have, you will notice small details that you hadn't noticed before, or that did not matter that much to you then, like fraying sheets and towels. It can be terrifying and depressing now, not to be able to afford new sheets and towels when before you could. When the only music you hear in the house is from the kiddie shows on television, when there is no one to have sex with tonight and you begin to feel like a woman who is untouchable, when you are the only one who empties the dishwasher, takes out the garbage, and puts the laundry away, when you realize that all of your friends are couples, you are feeling some of the unpleasant, depressing effects of marital separation.

You have reached a point where you can look back on a panorama of retrospection, on your regrets and the things that could not come to pass as you wanted them to. It will hurt as you receive this disheartening news, in addition to the discomfort you feel from your present situation, but you will also feel the relief of not having to fight against the tide of events anymore. You will not have to compete on a daily basis against the knowing, and you will be able to leave the struggle behind and go with the flow. If you can be patient, your discomfort lessens as you learn to accept yourself for your humanness, and your past as a part of your life. Being able to look back on the past and accept it helps you to see your future more clearly. If you can avoid becoming dismantled by desperation and loneliness, bite the bullet and accept your challenges now, especially the ones that seem to keep popping up at always the wrong times, you can start over without the same old bitterness and anger from your life before, when you were really desperate and lonely. A life lived with no failures to learn from is a life with no growth or expectations. It is a life lived solely for entertainment and an invariable, uneventful life.

We take ourselves wherever we are. Mileage doesn't do a thing to help us to escape. We carry everything in our hearts, and work things in and work things out, wherever we happen to be. When our baggage is on the lighter side, we have a better chance to exist with the possibility of feeling blessed, rather than falling prey to a life of heaviness and dread. With each step ahead from here, you will need to reevaluate the reasons why you left.

Over and over again. You will constantly look for affirmations for those reasons and you will find some. There will be times when you find nothing as well. Then, you have to put your trust in blind faith until the next positive and encouraging road sign appears. In the meantime, you can take comfort in the stories and friendships of others who have taken this same path. You are not alone. You must allow this journey to fulfill itself gradually. What you do have, for sure, and it's like money in the bank, is the spirit of yourself. Each day that you continue to grow and fulfill your promise to yourself, more and more of that is filling itself up inside of you.

Preparation and Planning

"Now, we're not talking about a reserve trust fund here. I think it's important for you to have put aside enough for you (and any children) to survive for at least three months once you know the relationship is tenuous, at best. You should have already looked into setting up a checking or savings account, and have investigated the possibilities in the job market."

Neal Olshan, PhD, Golden Handcuffs

One inexorable truth that can hit very hard is the fact that you have been financially dependent on your spouse, and maybe you still are. This is a barren wasteland for you to find yourself in. You may look at your surroundings for what you actually own and see very little or nothing. Rather than fall into an abyss of self-pity and hopelessness, embarrassment and low self-esteem, gear up to the task of finding a way to earn enough money for you. Whatever job you take to get you through this time to survive for the good of yourself and for the good of your children, you must know that it is only a vehicle to get you where you want to go. You do not have to define yourself by your occupation now that you are defining yourself by you.

Money can be the strongest connection that you have to your spouse right now. You might feel tethered around the waist to the man holding the rope at the top of the mountain. It can be up to him to pull you up or send you falling. Money, that old thing, has the potential to keep us subservient, weak, and childlike. We are reminded by money how much control it actually has over our own lives. Whenever we want to exercise our own free will, and we see lover boy over there waving the checkbook at the front door, we pull the car right back into the driveway again.

Some unhappy people manage to stay in a marriage because it would be too expensive for them not too. And that's all right if it works for them. We should never judge them. People instinctively know their limits and know how much about their lives they can change comfortably. It is hard for many women to break out of the cultural and societal boundaries that they are thrown into when they become wives, so they make the choice to hang in there for economic survival.

Families take on an enormous burden of financial responsibility to keep up with what society says we must own to be cool. Giving some of that up is not an option. Many people have become severely dependent on these things. Although some husbands might be quite aware that their salary is what has become the most attractive thing about them to their wives, they might emotionally dismiss that fact and find acceptance with the situation for practical reasons. Alimony and child support can be expensive. Who wants to go live in an apartment when you are used to a house? Who wants to have to do his own laundry and cook his own meals? Who wants to live alone, away from one's children? Who wants the marriage to end anyway? It is a heartbreaking event for the entire family.

If you find yourself at the point where you would rather live in a cardboard box with a battery operated lamp rather than live with your spouse for another minute, you need to think about how you are going to fill up your own purse.

When I physically separated from my husband, money became very important. It took the place of all issues for a good long while until I could break out of the place of not having enough. Although I had child support coming in, and for the first two years of my separation I received a limited alimony, which paid the rent for my daughter and me and nothing else, I had to be aware of every single penny that I spent. When you have children, you can depend on all sorts of unexpected expenses turning up. On some days, especially towards the end of the month, not having enough money became very scary for me. Of course, it didn't help when my ex-husband took his sweet time in getting the check to us, but helping us in this way was not on his agenda, and withholding money from us, even for a few days, gave him back some of the control that he had lost. At the time, if the child support check was a few days late it mattered. Month after month, I was often put into the excruciating position of begging for something that I was entitled to. At least I received a child support check every month, unlike many separated and divorced women, who have to dismiss the weak laws that enable some of the real deadbeats who don't pay child support while they are driving around in brand new cars. These women carry on alone or nobody eats and gets clothed today. Luckily, I found a small but dependable income by writing a weekly column for a neighborhood newspaper. When that wasn't enough, and it wasn't, I cooked for people and gave cooking lessons. The money that I earned from doing these things took the edge off my newly found reduced circumstances. I was determined not to let my daughter feel the punishment of money being withheld from us because I finally became fed up to here with all of the infuriating dysfunction that had sickened me to the point where I had to escape for my life and hers. But back there somewhere it would have pleased some people to no end if I had starved to death without their help.

Money, no matter where it comes from, can indeed be used as a tool to punish and to control, as it so often is. But it is important to realize that people who use their money in this way have nothing else except their money and that is very sad. The tattered cloak of embarrassment and insecurity that you are forced to wear now, as you suddenly lose what had been provided for you and your children before you ran out on the poor boy, is also a way for others to inflict punishment and revenge upon you. By not letting yourself be controlled in any way by other people's money, you break the connection that you have to them so that you can continue to advance on your journey to freedom. Earn your own and continue to work at being a separate you. Treat what help you do get from others as a surprise and you will not feel angry and disappointed when you do not get any.

When I could emerge momentarily through my fears about poverty, concerns about money brought clarity to my thoughts and to my emotions. Sometimes this more positive outlook would extend out to my actually enjoying the challenge of seeking out my little jobs to make ends meet. I was doing something for me. My choice to stay at home to be a writer, to be in the neighborhood to pick my daughter up from school everyday, and to be able to stay home with her when she was sick, without the panic that I would be fired, was something that I never regretted for a minute, even when I could not afford to buy my savored organic grapes at the market, and much more. I was sorry at times that I didn't have an MD or a degree in law, or any dependable income, so I could take her to Club Med for spring break, so we could have a car and live in a bigger place. It would have been nice to have my own bedroom instead of sleeping in the living room. But I found myself feeling so often like I would have cleaned toilets to support us, and loved it for the freedom it gave me. I would groove on my blessings while scrubbing away and listening to music on my walkman for the privilege of becoming free from the thick anguish and desolation of trying to live and raise a child in an unhappy home. This was my choice.

It might not happen overnight, but getting into the habit of believing that you can survive through this time actually becomes a habit and a real good one; one that can enable you to overcome your difficulties during this transition and take you far beyond it, into your future with confidence, light, and most important, an ability to be independent.

You might even realize that you have the ability to get through life, to get up every morning and function, even when you have a lot of things on your mind. When you release yourself from the image of a freeloader and from someone who can't, you become someone who is able to live each day, as the seed of freedom and independence grows inside of you. When you are offered a chance to reinvent yourself, you are given an opportunity to start over. This is a gift to be opened at once. You are beginning a new life with a good investment, the courage of your convictions. The power of that will always be there to help you.

Besides helping you to become more financially independent and secure, a job - any job - can help you to get out into a world that you might have been shut out from for longer than you would like to remember. You might actually discover that you are really good at something, no matter what it is, and your own special talents might contribute something worthwhile to the world out there. The good feedback that comes back to you from such a gratifying connection to the universe affirms where you are going.

If you have been out of touch with the work force for a while, it might feel dreadful at first, like the first day of school. And your new shoes might hurt too. Keep in the front of your mind what your main objective is. Try to have fun. Look back from where you have emerged and respect yourself for that.

> *"If we do not find anything very pleasant, at least we shall find something new."*
> Voltaire, French philosopher, Candide

Don't crawl into the closet now. The challenge of life on your own and facing the prospects of getting involved in something new, meeting new people, and finding yourself in a new environment can be motivating and can remind you that you are still alive. Give something a chance to develop.

Make a list:

Things that you can do in the closet:

1.

Things that you can do out of the closet:

1. through 100.

★

Although many fears about money can be irrational, your fears about money now are very real because you have changed the dynamics of the system. Once I could go a little over on my budget at the supermarket, or more likely on clothes. It didn't really matter as far as our financial survival was concerned, and it wasn't really such a big deal. If anything, I would be scolded and I couldn't wear the dress in his presence anymore. There was once a time when that certain someone would buy me something that I needed or wanted now and then. Even when I had to petition for it, it came to me paid for already. If we needed something for the house, we bought it. If the car broke down, the car got fixed. Since he was the breadwinner, I relaxed about counting every single one of my pennies that I earned. With the breakup of my marriage, he was gone and he took his wallet with him. Now it was all up to me. I was the boss man now.

Many women on their own worry constantly about not having enough money, and fears of becoming homeless and destitute are paralyzing. These worries cause us again to feel exasperated that we have no control over our own lives. We face concerns about how we will care for our children and how to give them good childhoods, so much so that it is hard for us to rest and so we worry about staying well for them too. So many of us are familiar with the panic caused from fear of lack of money because what we are up against is actually real, not imagined, and quite large. We know how difficult life can be for our class. It is essential to get through the terror and face the facts. Write them down if you have to. Know and accept how much money you have, how much you will need, and if necessary, how you are realistically going to attain it. Make a plan way in advance if you have to. Do not feel guilty about preparing yourself financially now for what you might be up against sooner or later.

It isn't easy to live with not enough money. While some of the world flaunts it and seems to be having a grand old time, you have to get back to the basics again. Your limited finances can be hard to manage when you are separated and solely responsible for paying the bills. You feel weakened along with your bank account. You often have to find the energy from an unknown inner reservoir, along with the ancient wisdom of Moses, to explain to your hypnotized children why they cannot have and should not have as many things as their friends do. Sometimes this is too great a load to bear, and you might regret your decision, yet again, to physically separate from your husband. You might justify going back to him just so your kids can have more toys.

When we are frightened about money, we loose a lot of perspective on the rest of our circumstances. The gloom that sets in when you see your bank account go way down before your next check comes in can set you back into a state of depression and have you reduced into running back to the life and the land where you left, to the place where he knows he has you.

*

Once, survival might have meant staying silent, saying thank you very much, and feeling eternally grateful for every little thing that was given to you. That might have been the plan. After a time of being made a prey for this indoctrination, you gradually become a suckered recipient, tip toeing and bowing down to all this control. What happens to you then, is that it becomes very difficult to break away from that pattern of behavior. You fear being shut out and punished because of, and with, your poverty, so you stay a thankful beggar, doing a beggar's dance. Looking back at this scenario, it is not that you were ever poor of money or self-worth, but of the spirit and confidence to know that you could go out and find it for yourself.

Often when we are married, we are used to neglecting ourselves because we are too busy taking care of everyone else's needs, past, present, and future. We just put ourselves last for some reason; we always have because it works so well and everything runs so smoothly when we do. We are so good. We feel nervous when we do begin to shape our own lives, just in case someone catches us doing it. God forbid that they will shake a pointed finger at us and accuse us of failing in our duty. We will almost never say, yes, we are failing in our duty to ourselves.

Sometimes we don the boxing gloves and jump into the ring to obtain what we want for ourselves. The fight is usually a wow knockout and when we win, and those of us who use this ploy usually do, the reward we demand for our stunning, drag-down performance is not only the thing we wanted and fought for, but also absolution of the guilt we felt in wanting it in the first place.

And some of us just run away. We do not suffer through the work and hope for someday. We do not fight for what we want so we can stay in the game. We just take a job that demands most of our time, go out a lot, or we stay in absentia, zonked out on one thing or another, still denying ourselves what we might really want, and denying others us.

When you are truly your own person, you feel authorized to take the time to learn how to design your life for the present and for the future. You do not have to hide your plan from anyone or fight for permission to attempt it. When this freedom is felt in a healthy way, and exercised with balance, the idea that you are deceiving anyone or stealing anything from them is someone else's agenda.

★

When I could feel that the rightness of my decision to separate was without a doubt, I felt entitled to ask for help when I really needed it, mainly because it concerned my daughter. When turned down a number of times from those who easily had either the ability or the money to help my daughter and me, I fell into a ghastly hole of anger and resentment. Again, I had to learn that on this journey there are countless discoveries to unearth. In my case, they were hidden, under layers of a life that I lived in a country where I did not belong.

You can explode in anger every time your spouse withholds financial support from you and the children, but the experience that comes back to enrage you again and again on a monthly basis risks becoming a vehicle for hatred. It can feel like you are still married to the guy. At some point, you have to let go of this unrelenting emotional struggle when you feel connected in this way. This can go on and on for years because it's such a good thing to fight about. Consider what you have to put yourself through to win. Try your best at obtaining what you deserve and let the rest go so you can get on with your life. Being prepared for this financially and emotionally, knowing with whom you are dealing with, and setting a legal precedent beforehand can protect you from this sometimes.

When money means more than just a means of paying bills for your spouse, it may become that kind of a larger emotional issue for you. If your relationship with your husband shrinks down to one where money is the only thing left for you to discuss, it naturally may also become the only thing left to fight about. Yuck. Although subconsciously, you both may feel sad or angry from this, it can be exhausting when you have to deal with someone who likes to control you with money in this way. Things could get pretty horrific if asking for money and stating the reason why you need it is constantly being twisted into an excuse for him to blame you for being the cause of his discomfort. If you can stay with the fact that you are just doing your job, raising your children and needing to obtain from their father what they honestly need, you can try to remain out of the entrapment of money issues that automatically pull you back in to a dysfunctional relationship. Let business just be business.

If, and after we realize, that we have been caretakers and martyrs for the love of others, and decide to change this for ourselves, we begin to grow up and into ourselves with clear, rational thinking and a calmer approach. We are not afraid to ask for what we want, nor are we afraid to depend on ourselves either. Let the no's come from the outside and from all sides. You should be ready to evaluate them, let your emotional attachments to them go out the window, and transform some of them yourself into feasible possibilities.

For any successful endeavor, goals and expectations that are realistic serve us better than fantasies or ideas based only on our emotions. When you do begin to depend on yourself more, you need to take care of yourself more. It is essential for you to try your best to stay well, mentally and physically. It is important to stay in reality and to always try to remember to stay balanced.

We sometimes forget that we can be loved for our strengths and our abilities to take care of ourselves, rather than for our need to be taken care of, or for our talent to take care of others. It is a different relationship with the world when this is true. When you lose the nurturing from others - that nourishment that you thought you so desperately needed and maybe you did, and the things that the nurturing brought to you - you are either able to let go of the attachment to these things and move on, or you become stuck to them.

★

Developing into yourself without much money allows you to stop needing so many things. There are the basics, of course and the extras and perks that make life worth living, but you must not jeopardize you and your children financially. Besides, the landfills are already over flowing. The spaces inside of you are also filled up to the brim with the wrong things, if you continue to define yourself by your possessions. From refusing to give in to this, you clear the way for the unfolding of the invaluable you. To avoid getting caught in the vacuum of materialism is a challenge, especially in this society of charging consumerism. If you win, you move from living outside of yourself to living in the inside of you. As it turns out, you can live life of a better quality when the fickle and fleeting spirit of "I want" is put in its place.

When money is an issue, it can enable you to avoid the other emotions that you are feeling and are afraid to confront. *So, all of your problems would go away if you just had that house, huh?* Lack of money causes us to feel our separation and our loss in the most intense way. It represents everything you need right now if you let it. Inanimate objects cause you to have false confidence while you neglect what truly matters. In this place, you can be tempted to ignore your true feelings for the convenience of using material things to give you that much needed break from what is actually happening to you. Unfortunately, when you and your possessions become inseparable and they take on an emotional significance, inanimate objects speak instead of you.

What is your alternative? Starve for the sake of you? The further you go on this journey, the more separated you become, and as each step you take is careful, things can seem more complicated, but hopefully more evolved and simpler too. There is a harmony that we can achieve based on our own circumstances and our own goals. Since each woman's situation is different, it is up to her to find a reasonable place where she can focus on growing, a place where she can resist hopelessness and despair, and still have fun.

Collecting handbags and shoes will not take us out of our dilemmas for long, even when we look fabulous. Besides, who has the room? We accumulate these wonderful things and as much as some of us would hate to admit, not so wonderful things, so they fall out on our heads when we open the closet, or we see them lying all over the place because the closets are filled. And then, to make our preoccupation more evident, it all goes out of style next year, so we need to get some more. This heaping up is constantly reminding us of how glued we are to this state, yet we continue to ignore the blatant message. Have what you need so you can feel that you look great, then move on from being stuck in the state of how you look into the real confidence that helps you to actually get out there and function.

This entire journey is a letting go and moving on process. In order to move forward on this journey, we have to let go of so much of what we think we would rather hold on to. Obsessions about how we look, obsessions about what we possess, and obsessions about what we want others to think about us are places where we can put off our emptiness and be on vacation. It can be like living in a luxury hotel, with a shopping mall downstairs, a spa on the roof, and a gambling casino which pumps in oxygen to keep us going night and day.

When we mistakenly act out our most sincere needs in these obsessions, we need to take back the power of want in us in a different way, check out of that land of luxury and go home. We need to reevaluate our needs for survival when we lose ourselves in shortcuts, which lead to nowhere, and delay ourselves for the sake of buying another day.

Loss of things can be painful. It can feel like a progression of amputations, watching the things that we crave and identify with pass us by on the way to the so-called Promised Land. For a very long time, I was under the impression that the things that I coveted would solve my problems. The more that I pined for them, the more important to my life they became. What I found out when I finally received the things that I gave false power to, was that there were more and more things out there waiting their turn, saying take me home! This was not the way to myself.

In order to move on with your life, you must put wealth into equal portions of your pie. Money isn't everything. We need it to survive, we must have it to survive, but it is not all that we need to grow, to be happy, and raise happy, well-loved children. When you prepare yourself for a life separate, you need to know how to change your environment in a way that gives you not only what you need to survive economically, but emotionally as well.

*

You need to know how to protect yourself from falling into the pull of rampant consumerism in the disguise of a discount or a great bargain. It adds up, especially when shopping takes the place of doing something else, something more worthwhile. To continue on this journey safely and realistically, we need to ask ourselves if our needs can be met in other ways, besides by spending on things that we cannot afford. What part of us is falsely being taken care of when we accumulate these empty promises with our hard earned cash and take them home?

If you really need to care about your finances now, and how you are going to survive on your own, you need to be aware of how you spend your money and where your money goes. We are a society that is sold on solutions we can buy, instead of learning to solve things in other ways. If you can get to the point where you can find fulfillment and solutions to your problems in other ways besides shopping and accumulating, you will be able to survive through situations that cause you to buckle down without compromising too much of your emotional well-being.

After a time of practicing a different approach to sustaining yourself through the conspicuous fact that you are on your own, there comes the joyfully surprising realization that people can live well with very little of what society tells them to buy. Issues about your finances and your economic survival, now that you can see clear of the rush for material accumulation, are more clear, more outside of you and less self-centered. If you have children, you need to think about the future and the kind of world that they will inhabit when you are gone. You should pay attention to where your money is actually going now since you are the one paying the bills, and more than that, you are the one who can instigate a transformation. The result of this struggle is in your finally emerging out of the shadows of the broom closet and into the wide-open spaces of someone who can make a difference.

The journey through to real change and self-renewal can be a hard and frightening passage. It seems like we have to give up so much to gain so little at the beginning. Some women may have nothing else to move on with but faith. Whether we are responsible for our children traveling with us or just for ourselves, we desperately want to reach our destination safely and as fast as we can, so we can finally let go of this process, and it can feel like the road never ends. Whenever and however we do finally get there, we always begin by starting from where we are.

Separation and Uncertainty

"There comes a time in our lives when we are called to believe the unbelievable. If we allow ourselves to believe, we open the door to the ultimate possibility of who we might become."

*Ann Linnea, Deep Water Passage,
A Spiritual Journey at Midlife*

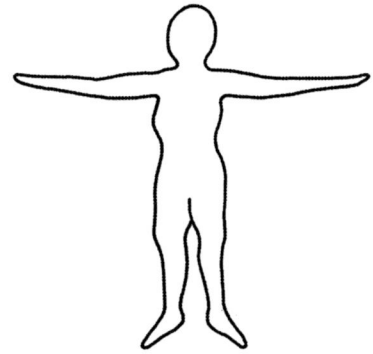

The new life that you sought to discover when you embarked on this journey is only just beginning. When you finally get to this point, stop for a moment or two to appreciate the courage that it took for you to launch yourself out and off into who knows where. That courage and the stamina that you might not have known you had, will continue to help you on the paths that you follow for the rest of your life. Your commitment to your goals has paid off in the fact that you are here. Nobody said that it was going to be easy, but someone did say that anything worth its salt never is. We become our own heroes every day that we succeed in living as us.

After my divorce and my remarriage, I still have concerns that take me back into this book and cause me to return to the journey over and over again.

The influence that you summon to help you towards your destination can come from many different places, and you can develop a sense of security from having what inspires you come from a good and worthy source of enrichment because you will know where to find it. You will know if the reassurances and encouragements are coming from the right place by how you feel. If it is hard to know how you feel, it is usually because you are stuck in something that you still need to learn from, perhaps by being too emotionally attached to the things that you need to let go of.

Although you might be chomping at the bit by now to set off to live in your own new nation, and all of the affirmations that appear on a daily basis while you carry on with your hard work fills you with a sense of entitlement, *to please get you there already,* take heed. Study the map carefully before venturing forth. You have a pretty solid history of experience behind you, where you know what is expected of you and what to expect from others. You are familiar with that landscape and its inhabitants, and you understand and speak the language, because that is where you came from. Amidst reinventing yourself now and growing up, there may be some surprises and unforeseen wildernesses for you to maneuver through unexplored open country.

Our own attitude about ourselves can mean everything sometimes, especially in the bleakest of circumstances. Sometimes the definition of ourselves is all we have to support ourselves with, because even though we are sure that our friends will stay our friends through thick and thin, we are wrong. So, we end up not only losing a husband, a marriage, perhaps custody of our children, but sadly, we might lose friends as well. Something happens to people who refuse to listen and grow up. They become sad caricatures of themselves as they desperately try to avoid moving into an adult state of mind. They will blame you for things that are outside of your responsibility because they are still stuck in blaming the outside for everything that they haven't been given in life. They won't be bothered to do the work on themselves to get out of that infantile state. And if you have indeed grown up or are on your way, you become the parent to their child and the relationship changes. Unfortunately, you might have to go through some rather unpleasant mini divorces from selfish, hollow people of limited access, who we once thought would surely be attending our children's weddings.

All of the work towards separating from that which brings you down helps you to learn how to avoid attaching yourself to every thing that comes flying in your direction. And it will come flying in your direction. We cannot insulate ourselves from the ways of the world, but by focusing on moving out of the way of those who feel that they have an ax to grind, and escaping those who will undoubtedly drag you down to enable them in their afflictions and addictions, you can achieve some confidence in your choice of to whom you want to give even an ounce of your attention. Does this sound snobby and indifferent? Compare your life connected to people who assassinate your character and suck you dry for their own agenda to living with those who don't.

When you become aware of your own weakness and susceptibility to people who have always seemed to pick you to leach onto emotionally, they finally lose their touch. Even your mother cannot ruin it for you. Even she might have to be left alone with her own opinions. In separating from mother, do we dare to exist at all?

A point of view that sees your daily glass of poison as almost empty, and retreating back to the things in your life that really count is what nourished you when you felt empty and defeated. This is what will continue to replenish you with what you need to get through the rest of your life. It is the only real thing that will get us through our losses.

Forget about removing yourself completely from life's challenges and unpleasantness. That is not why we are here. We are meant to approach and embrace all of life, including its meanness and terribleness, rather than blow ourselves up in defense of it all. We exist in this world with the worst of it and we take a part in living in it too. We contribute our own failings to this world, even if they are tiny in comparison to the rest. It is going in the wrong direction if we judge it all so we can fall under the misconception that we are outside of it. If we do not accept life's whole package, we will never learn to understand and learn to do something about life's challenges, and neither will our children.

If you are afraid of repeating an old pattern of behavior, or feel yourself actually falling back into one, the fact is that if you can see it coming, it is a good thing and you are probably well on top of it. It is a realistic notion that a repeat performance, of what you staged back then and there with you know who, can present itself as an option. Take care of you. You made the choice not to sleepwalk through the rest of your life. You committed yourself to waking up from a life of denial or a life of bad dreams. That decision makes its impact in the form of a new life that you have the power to do something about.

✶

    Finally discovering that you own some power over your life can make you feel a tad bit nervous, and you might inflict yourself with guilt as an antidote to this sudden feeling of actually being in control and responsible for making things happen. Every time that you do something about your life, it changes you. Expect results when you put your foot down and insist on keeping separate from the forces that are driving you crazy. What do you do with your assertive self now? Start with an end to the labeling - as a bitch or someone less than adequate. You should know better than that now because you have reached a point where you understand only too well where that stuff comes from. You should also quit blaming every one for causing you to feel bad and accept responsibility for yourself already, and move on.

As well as some surprises and new awakenings, separation and uncertainty can bring disappointment, which can be especially painful if you thought that you were finally beyond the lessons. We want to be recognized by others now in the ways that we recognize ourselves. Unfortunately, women are still labeled with derogatory names when they stand up and fight for what they think is right, even by other women. When they assert themselves on how things stand, even if they are wrong, and when they have to vociferate their opinions over the voices of the ones putting them down just because they are women, these brave ones are at risk for an unfair mark of identification. Even when she is applying herself to keeping things sane and even, there are those who will automatically look for her weaknesses, and place an agenda on a woman as a stigma against her because she is speaking with self-assurance. It is not that we, as a society, have not evolved enough to move beyond this form of ignorance. We could if we really wanted to. If we can take ourselves out of the emotional struggle long enough to observe some of the reactions we incite, we would realize that giving women the credibility that they deserve - and would live up to if allowed - would leave too many people with nothing to say. Their noise would no longer bring about our silence.

After a time, I became used to not knowing what kind of response from the outside world to expect towards me now as a single mother with my own power. I was branded by all these different impressions. Living in the land of being consistently stumped by people's reactions towards me became possible only after I accepted myself as the woman who I wanted to be. Whatever feedback I received after I felt comfortable with myself became superfluous. Some of the responses dished out towards me, that I can laugh about now, ranged from really strong concerns about whether I was in therapy - and probing questions about why not - to people who ran to get their coats, to position themselves at the door for a quick getaway from what was invented in their own minds as the sorrow and the pity. When you get to the place where you can take in, know how to forgive, and embrace life's misfires and clownish behavior, life is truly marvelous, isn't it? It's like a movie.

After the grand tour like the one that I just returned from, I emerged as someone who was not going to take any crap from anyone anymore. It showed. It had to show its ugly face, considering all of the disappointments that I was experiencing at the time. I would like to think that I was not too mean or too intolerant. It absolutely depended on with whom I was dealing. Psychos, nutcases, and narcissists didn't stand a chance. I tried to come across with the yin and yang in me well balanced, but it still hurt my feelings when I interacted with people who did not even know me and would not even give me a chance. But I always said, well, I made it this far, and I went back to the source of my pleasures and bliss, back to my loved ones, back to my real friends, and always found my way again.

This is your land, dear voyager. If you can take an outsider's interest in watching life unfold before you, you release yourself from the day-to-day worry that you will be misunderstood and punished for venturing forth, even when you veer off course. You can finally stop living from one unpleasant experience to another. You can let go of the trepidation and fear from false alarms, move through, and move on.

The discovery of your present state, this one where you have ended up after walking away from a life that you were so frightened of giving up for so long, heals. Getting this far on your journey means that you no longer have to feverishly hold in your concealed nature to hold on to your past. Even after years and years of putting up with being told things about you that were someone else's wrong interpretations and impressions, you can recognize that you hid away from it all and now you are brave enough to come out to see the reasons why you hid yourself away. Who wouldn't hide from this type of psychological imprisonment?

Once, you depended on others for things you can now reclaim as your own, such as power, resourcefulness and creativity. Those negative stereotypes of strong women that kept you from becoming one, fade into the past now, as you let go and escape to become the woman that you want to be.

✷

Those poor souls who mope about in the shadows of your atmosphere, and hang around your aura, affected by your so-called selfishness, and begrudging your progress, are not telling you much, except how they feel. If we trust ourselves with the choices we make, if we truly believe in our true natures from the glimpse of ourselves that we have been lucky enough to receive so far, we can pass that faith in us on to others we really care about in a positive way.

Sometimes I could lift myself out of my situation to consider the feelings of people who I knew to be loyal and reasonably sane, no matter how infantile or self-centered their behavior seemed to be. Often, their acting out was a cry for help. If you can make a distinction between the people who matter and the ones who don't, you can comfortably avoid reacting to their baited hooks to catch you at causing their unhappiness. After all, and this is important to remember, we still have family and extended family. We still have bosses, co-workers, and people with whom we associate for whatever reason. With some people, it is worth the effort to try to get them to eventually back off and stop trying to get you to bite their smelly old bait.

As expected, that approach failed to work for me with some people. In order to please them, I would have had to return to my past life and stay there to enable them. Since that was absolutely out of the question for me, I had to hold my ground, drop my last hope, and relinquish the task.

We often edit ourselves for the sake and convenience of others. That is fine if it is done out of consideration of other's feelings. When we cannot stop burying ourselves in their needs, we suffocate our lives in someone else's problems. They are breathing our air. If we can take that energy back and put it into ourselves, where it belongs, we can start to breathe again.

It is a risky business to begin to be oneself. You never know whether you are saying yes, or if you are saying no to someone else's pleas. Your attention is focused on you rather than on them, so you may not be aware of the fact that you might be giving them the wrong answer until someone calls it to your attention. Do not start to berate yourself for not seeing through the blur and fog of the outside world and its needs right away. You have only just learned to become nearsighted enough to focus on your own needs.

If you have children and a family, their needs might be demanding most of your attention. Friends and new relationships might want more of you for whatever the reason. So, what do you do now, as the pressure of being there begins to feel like a negative, impossible assignment? Just listen. Allow the voices to tell you how they feel, and what they need. Hear these pleas from the place where they originate. Then, remember what your priorities are. Do not be afraid to be misjudged or judged at all. Who is doing the judging? You are the judge of yourself now. You need to know that there is an impact on others when you have moved on to this change. You either become a role model and one who is respected, or you turn into a walking pariah who awakens all the insecurities of others.

When you disconnect from what was bringing you down, you also disconnect from a lot of things that once fit so well into the old, wayworn style of your past. Sometimes you become stuck in the unpleasant state of departure, and cannot leave and get away. You find yourself returning to ring the doorbell just "one mo time!" to receive some more punishment from the ones who think that you are abandoning them with no cause, again and again. It serves them to put the blame on you, and it serves you to keep thinking that they are bad. When this happens, it is best to just say see ya, get yourself outside of that negativity, and stop trying to apologize for leaving. Stop asking for their blessing. Stop trying to get them to change. Sometimes, with some people, you just need to go.

✶

By now, the longest, most intense time of struggling with your feelings has hopefully ceased, but each and every one of your emotional chapters will overlap and continue to compete for your attention, sometimes all at once, because life does not occur in nice, clean, orderly stages. If the dust has indeed settled a bit, you might find room for some philosophic meditation and reflection on the loss of what kept you attached. This is when I could tell my daughter that I missed Daddy sometimes.

After I finally arrived to this place on my journey, I found that I could eventually look back on my marriage with an old and rather uncomfortable feeling of sentimentality. At first, I could not understand what my thoughts were doing and I felt like I was weakening. What happened to dropping the whole disastrous experience like a hot potato, the name calling, forgetting about those so-called wasted years at war and moving on? Now, that my hardest work of feeling confused and angry had passed, after all of my crying and feelings of tragic loss, and having come to believe to the utmost that I know what the bottom of the barrel looks and feels like now, now I was sorry?

It hurts to lose a husband. This guy, who was once such a large part of your life, is, poof, suddenly gone. It takes time to exorcise the feeling from yourself that you do not belong to him anymore. In his absence, you might feel bombarded by his larger than life memory, and it can be a long time before his affect on your life eases off. But when some of us do lose our husbands, it is at this moment that we step over the threshold and into the thing that is urging us on. We feel it, as life becomes fragile and mysterious, because we have moved into somewhere alone without them. Everyday, we are reminded of how much we have been touched by our moving away because the memories have become a part of our life, whether we like it or not.

In time, we do enter a new place, where the past becomes less upsetting and hindering, because we draw on the energy of our new life. As you become stronger and more independent of the old connections, the image of the one you separated from may shock you, as they appear older, shorter, fatter, thinner, richer, poorer, balder, happy or sad. They might feel separate from you now, and you will become conscious of that when you see them wearing a shirt that you do not recognize. We might banish them faraway into a place where they are shunned, rather than see them this way, as they are now. When someone, who we once felt very deeply about and attached to, again touches us, from where we stand today, we might be afraid to feel that in growing up we have become more human than we ever wanted to be, or thought we ever could be.

We often try to stay connected to our husbands by defining them as babies, jerks, and fools. This works for us when we are still like children playing house. He's a dope; she's a shrew. It's just like on television! When we can grow up and no longer be attached to each other in this negative way, we can begin to see men as our equals, and just as imperfect as we are. We become a part of the great life long struggle together. Unfortunately, it often takes a journey such as this one as a catalyst for understanding that kind of connection, and by now, at least for our past relationship, it is too late.

I think that people want to remain in control of things all the time, just in case. I think that people think that life will play a cruel trick on them if they begin to relax and stop listening for the bullet. This is an ongoing theme between people these days. We forget how to say thank you. Eventually, and before we know it, we become way beyond each other's grasp when we are this way.

✶

We need to go through a time that feels uncomfortable, like we have traveled on too long a road, making leeway only by one step at a time, venturing way too far in the rain and snow with holes in our shoes, when we become reborn into ourselves. The possibility that we might not have made it intensifies this journey even more. We need to feel tired from it and say whew! Many of us have had to evacuate with everything we owned on our backs to an unknown land because the place where we lived became forbidding and inhospitable. Our discomfort now is from having to take in and try to understand so much of what we saw on our journey, of our disheartening discoveries, and of having to find the strength to steel ourselves to uncover the good things as well. We need to feel this way now so that we can remember.

Someday, we may need to show our children a way to go on. Right now, everything that we have ever gone through in our lives is in our memories so we can show them how to live. Before we face our growing up with the harsh reality of growing old, we must know that our children give us an opportunity to correct things. If we can get over our pain of having been mistaken and misunderstood, named by our nearest and dearest by all the wrong definitions, or otherwise just totally held aloof, we can let all of it go for the sake of becoming wise to it. Then, some of us can stop defining our daughters who ask for their needs to be met with the imperfection and inexperience of childhood as divas, drama queens, primadonnas, bookworms, tomboys, little bitches, rebels, spoiled brats, and you're just like your father.

If we continue the tradition of passing on negative attitudes with our children, we uphold the continuance of our pain from what has obviously hurt us the most in life, and we cut our own lives and our children's lives short of joy. When we show them how to ask for what they need and desire in a positive way, and fill them up with their right to it, we can put an end to our own painful struggle with coming to terms with our past as well.

When my old favorite pants didn't zip up when I finally squeezed myself into them, I automatically became depressed and thought that I had become fat. But I really was not fat. My body had changed. But I really wanted to get that goddamn zipper up on those pants. So, here were my options. I could keep them as a souvenir. I think of a time when I get to be seventy-nine, again, and I pull these sad, moth-eaten pants out of the vault and look at them (if I am lucky enough to remember what they are) and say what? Starving myself completely to fit into them was another way to go, but I knew that I could never do it just for a pair of old pants. I began to feel nauseated from the very thought of it. So, I figured that they make other pants, and I got rid of the ones that no longer fit.

The same thing can occur with old feelings. You may still want to fit into those feelings but their time has passed. The ones that have hung around you for what seems like a lifetime seem way too small now.

You have grown and expanded in the way that may find you changing how you accept things. Like fashion and styles of clothing, the feelings become dated, and don't say, "don't throw it out because it all eventually comes back someday" because even if it does come back, there is always something a little different, with a new twist about it. That is what keeps us optimistic. Too much vintage just looks like you are trying too hard to live in the past. It's too out of time for the present.

You really get to put in to practice the act of letting go now. It feels like so much needs to be shed. You can finally drop your expectations that everyone, even your ex-spouse, will change with your splendid reemergence. If he could not be what you wanted him to be when you were married, who says that he would meet you even halfway after you separate?

It could happen that you finally emerge in your new independent skin as the person that your spouse would have wanted you to be all along. In separating from him, you have grown up and learned to accept him for who he is.

★

We emerge from this experience finding out that it is possible to wear our broken hearts as badges because we can, and we own that right, but we can also find a way to heal and carry on, scars and all. We learn that we may go running back many times, in many different ways, with every possible excuse, to stay connected. This is to be expected when we finally accept the fact that the moving away from a husband is eventual and difficult.

Most of us end up just accepting the fact that we might have to continue to pick up the slack regarding the children, *and even though it says joint custody on the agreement,* the exes need to get laid or play with the guys this weekend, so they won't be around. Many women are on their own most of the time, trying to make ends meet, while their ex-spouses buy leather couches and go to the Bahamas. Feeling jealous about this just keeps you connected.

Once you might have been terrified of your spouse not getting it about you. Now it should not matter. You know who you are. You can accept what once was the darkness of not knowing, of being afraid and feeling insecure just as easy as it is for you accept the natural darkness of night now.

From this point, if you are lucky and smart, you realize that if you do the right thing the first time, regarding your ex and regarding your children, and act in a way that shows you to be reliable and old enough to know better, you will not have to repeat tasks to correct things, or look back at your poor conduct with regret. You begin to rely on the outcome of doing the right thing.

When my marriage was about to end finally with a physical separation from my husband, he came to me in our kitchen and asked me if there was anything that he could do to make me stay. This can seem like a normal, expected request, and I know that, for him, it was a last minute attempt at keeping things together. For me though, at that moment, it meant something different. After years of my desperately wishing for him to ask me what I wanted and needed, he finally did, at last.

Although I emerged through a time that was uncomfortably familiar to what a slow death might feel like, I found myself reborn into me. Little by little, I saw through the lessons, even when all hope had seemed to fail. I trusted in the outcome of this journey because of everything it had taught me, and when I stopped and looked around at my present surroundings, they always looked better than the place I felt determined to let go, even when I was afraid.

We start out on this journey needing help. Gradually, if we can become receptive and stay resilient, we find it and we can learn and grow. Then, we begin to believe that everyone needs protection because this is a frightening experience.

We cover our ears often so we cannot hear the explosions of another come-down. We tap dance on fashion runways, run endlessly on treadmills, and stay stuck in places that are messy and without compassion. We struggle in all sorts of ways to ease the pain of our injuries, abuses, and abandonment. We travel in the bad weather, on rocky roads and through deep dark tunnels of hatred to get away from it all. But then we emerge and receive it into our lives. When we get to a place on our journey where we can love others, we are ready to live. When we get to a place on our journey where we can love ourselves, we are ready to fly.

✱

About the Author

Denise Falcone is a writer who lives in New York City. Her practical education in marital separation and divorce began at an early age, when her parents split up in 1963. She took refresher courses when both of her parents second marriages also ended in divorce. When her own marriage became troubled, she found herself struggling with the process of separation from a more intensely personal point of view, and began looking for insight into how to deal with the powerful emotions she was feeling. Now, as a writer, she wants to share her insights so that more women might find this process, not just a traumatic, frightening experience, but also an opportunity for growth.

Printed in the United States
53626LVS00001B/225